Fido's Virginia

Barnabus is one of the black Labs that inspired Chateau Morrisette's Black Dog wines.

(Courtesy of the Roanoke Convention & Visitors Bureau)

Shiloh, the Blue Crab Bay Labradoodle, loves to go out on the boat with her mom.

(Courtesy of Blue Crab Bay)

Fido's Virginia

Ginger Warder

The Countryman Press
Woodstock, Vermont

Fido's Virginia
978-1-58157-148-6

Interior photographs by the author unless otherwise specified

Maps © The Countryman Press

Book design by S. E. Livingston

Book composition by Eugenie S. Delaney

Published by The Countryman Press, P.O. Box 748, Woodstock, VT 05091

Distributed by W. W. Norton & Company, Inc., 500 Fifth Avenue, New York, NY 10110

Printed in the United States of America

10 9 8 7 6 5 4 3 2 1

For my big sister, Judy Schroeder,
who is the queen of maps, a fun travel companion,
and knows every mile marker in the Old Dominion.

The Fox family's furry son, Diesel, loves to hike in the Blue Ridge Mountains.

Acknowledgments

With special thanks to the Virginia Tourism Corporation and especially photographer Bill Crabtree, who captured our cover dog, Jasper, as he said hello to a blue crab on Chapel Creek in Mathews County. Thanks also to all of the local canines and their humans who agreed to share their stories.

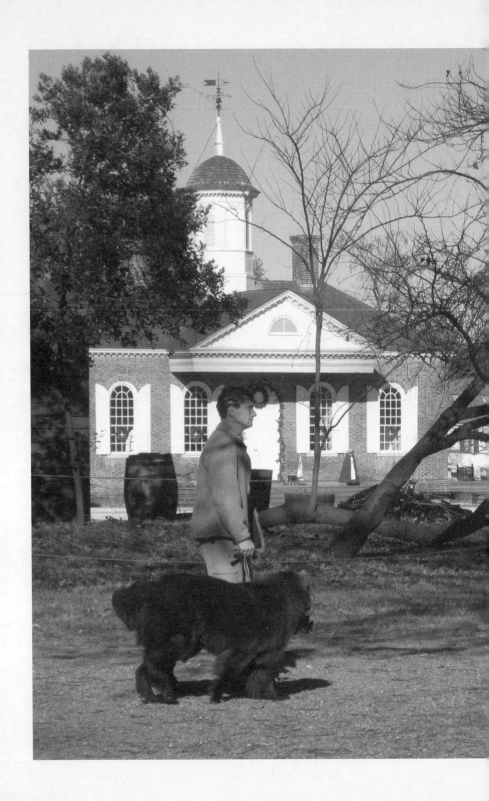

Contents

From the Author

I grew up on the Potomac River, just below George Mason's Gunston Hall Plantation and what is now a state park called Mason Neck. We sailed, canoed, and went waterskiing on the river, caught catfish and picked blackberries and went "chicken-necking" for crabs (dangling a piece of raw chicken on a string). I had a horse named Bay Rum, and we went foxhunting all over Northern Virginia and belonged to the Woodlawn Pony Club. If I close my eyes, I can still smell the honeysuckle that rioted in the summer and hear the frogs and crickets that sang every night outside my bedroom window. I have musket balls and arrowheads that I found in my own front yard, and I grew up seeing bald eagles and great blue herons along the river, along with wildlife from white-tailed deer to cottontail rabbits and groundhogs. I've traveled the state from one end to the other, often taking my great-nieces and -nephews along, to see the Old Dominion's historical sites and natural beauty through their eyes as well as my own. And of course, my loyal and constant four-legged companions (Cindy, Weezer, Tipsy, and Max) have filled my life and my journeys with furry fun.

Riding the Rails with Owney

In the late 1880s, a scruffy dog appeared one day in the Albany post office, and the clerks there named him Owney. The pooch had a fondness for riding in postal wagons and following mailbags onto trains. The railway mail service considered Owney to be their good-luck charm, and as he traveled the country, postal employees would affix tags and medals to his collar. Postmaster General John Wanamaker even gave Owney a special jacket to display his treasures. We're not sure what towns in Virginia Owney passed through, but today, his replica resides near Northern Virginia in the Smithsonian Institution's National Postal Museum in Washington, DC. You can learn more about Owney's life through his e-Book, *Owney: Tales from the Rails*, his iPhone app, and his special song, performed by country superstar Trace Adkins. And, of course, he has his own commemorative postage stamp!

(www.postalmuseum.si.edu/owneyapp).

Many visitors explore Colonial Williamsburg the way the original residents did: in a horse-drawn carriage.

You can't throw a rock in Virginia without hitting a historic site of some sort, since Virginia was the birthplace not only of the New World but also of America as we know it. I know there are significant attractions that are not included in this book: I've highlighted the most-visited areas and hope that readers will follow their own path in finding other interesting places in the state, many of which are easy day trips from the regions detailed here. Charlottesville is a convenient hub for exploring central Virginia, while Richmond anchors the region that includes the Eastern Shore and the Historic Triangle. The Shenandoah Valley is an easy drive from Northern Virginia, and Shenandoah National Park is easily accessible from there, as well as from many of the central and western destinations. Roanoke, in the heart of the Blue Ridge Mountains, is a perfect location for exploring the southwestern parts of the state.

I wanted to share my love of my home state and its distinct personality, which was shaped, in large part, by its role in America's history. I've included some of the most pet-friendly destinations and activities the Old Dominion offers, from stunning parks to somber battlefields, and I hope that you and your best friends will discover your own favorites along the way.

Introduction:
Virginia Is for Dog Lovers

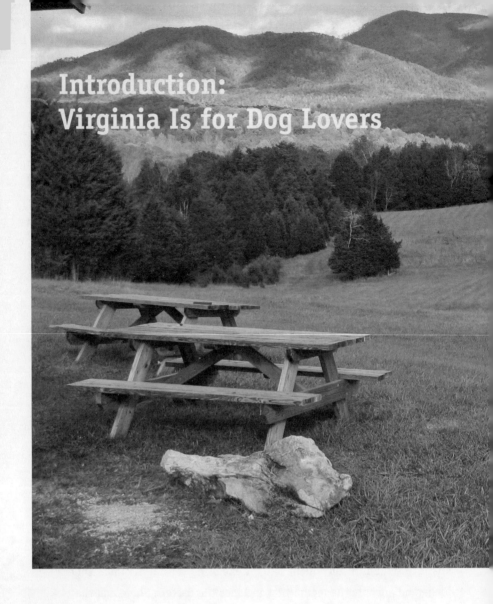

ocal canines like Jasper, our cover dog, helped with the travel research for *Fido's Virginia*, sniffing out the best of the Old Dominion for you and your best friends to explore. In addition to recommendations for the best places to stay and play, we've profiled several of the state's famous four-legged Virginians, including historic canines and living local legends. Since we're one of the few states to have an official state dog, one could say that Virginia is home not only to America's oldest colony but also to America's most historic dogs. In fact, it was George Washington who created Virginia's state dog, the American foxhound.

The spectacular view from Blue Ridge Vineyards.

Virginia is often called the birthplace of a nation, home to the first permanent settlement in the New World, at Jamestown, and to some of the most
famous orators and writers of the Revolutionary War. One of the original 13
states, Virginia is also known as the Mother of Presidents, since eight of the
nation's leaders hailed from the state: George Washington, Thomas Jefferson,
James Madison, James Monroe, William Harrison, John Tyler, Zachary Taylor,
and Woodrow Wilson. George Washington was born in the Northern Neck, had
strong ties to Fredericksburg, and loved his Alexandria estate on the Potomac
River, Mount Vernon. Thomas Jefferson designed some of the most prominent

Take your pooch for a historic stroll around the grounds of George Washington's Alexandria home, Mount Vernon. (Courtesy of the Virginia Tourism Corporation)

buildings in Virginia and influenced its architecture for centuries, introduced viticulture and gastronomy to the New World, and is one of the most revered Virginians in history for his innovations and ideals. Referred to as the War Between the States by most Southerners, the Civil War ended in Virginia, where more battles were fought than in any other state.

Old Dominion canines worked alongside the early colonists to carve out our country, fought alongside their humans in three wars, and are still an important part of Virginia's hospitality and history. Fidos throughout the state, like Sally at Black Dog Salvage in Roanoke, work alongside their humans and warmly welcome four-legged visitors to their businesses. One of the top vineyards in Virginia, Château Morrissette, not only welcomes furry visitors but also names its wines after the black dogs that inspired them. And while history is entwined with every square mile of the Old Dominion, Virginia also offers some of the nation's premier recreational areas, from Virginia Beach on the Atlantic Ocean to Shenandoah National Park in the western part of the state. For the most part, canines are considered to be

Virginiaisms

Virginia is one of four states that call themselves a commonwealth (Kentucky, Pennsylvania, and Massachusetts are also commonwealth states), a term derived from English common law. The tenth state to be admitted to the Union, Virginia's state flag bears the Commonwealth seal of the goddess Virtus, armed with a spear and sword and standing over a defeated tyrant, as well as the state motto, "Sic semper tyrannis," which means "Thus always to tyrants." Though today Virginia's tourism motto is "Virginia Is for Lovers," the state known as the birthplace of a nation was not hesitant to fight for its rights.

Both the state flower and the state tree are the dogwood; the state bird is the cardinal; and the state dog is the American foxhound. Virginia even has a state bat, the Virginia big-eared bat, as well as two state fish, the brook trout (freshwater) and striped bass (saltwater), and a state insect, the tiger swallowtail butterfly. And of course, there has to be a state song: adopted in 1940, James Bland's "Carry Me Back to Old Virginny" was re-named ("Virginny" changed to "Virginia") and redesignated as "song emeritus" in 1997.

Accents vary widely throughout the state, from the "non-accent" of Northern Virginians to the unique dialect spoken on isolated Tangier Island, which dates back to Elizabethan England. In the Tidewater area, Virginia becomes "Vuh-ginia," and in the southwestern corner of the state, a hint of Tennessee drawl creeps into Virginian speech.

family in Virginia—except, unfortunately, by the Commonwealth of Virginia's Health Department, which strictly prohibits all but service dogs from the premises of restaurants, including patios and decks.

Named for Queen Elizabeth I, the Virgin Queen, Virginia is as diverse as the colonists who settled here. The Blue Ridge Mountains define the western part of the state, home to one of the most popular national parks in America. Shenandoah National Park and scenic Skyline Drive draw thousands of visitors in the fall, when the mountain foliage is aflame with orange and red. In the summer, the park is filled with hikers and their four-legged friends, as leashed dogs are allowed on most trails as well as in campgrounds and cabins. The Blue Ridge Parkway also offers several scenic stopping points and recreational areas for canines and their companions.

Virginia State Code Prohibiting Animals in Restaurants

Only service dogs are allowed in restaurants and on their enclosed patios or decks, so dining out with Fido can be challenging. Some exceptions include take-out restaurants that have open areas (not enclosed) with picnic tables or outdoor seating, and small inns or B&Bs that house less than 18 guests. Pet-friendly hotels also have exemptions from some of these restrictions.

Northern Virginia is usually defined as a suburb of Washington, DC, but its western reaches are fertile ground for horse and dog lovers. You and your pooch can walk in the footsteps of George Washington on the gorgeous grounds of Mount Vernon or stroll on some of his favorite streets in historic Old Town Alexandria. Pooches can sink their paws in the sand of Virginia Beach, stroll through verdant vineyards, take a boat ride on one of the state's many rivers and lakes, or learn about their brave brethren on the battlefields of the Revolutionary and Civil Wars. King Charles II gave Virginia the moniker the Old Dominion in recognition of the colony's loyalty to the crown during the English Civil War, and the state's rich history makes it difficult to

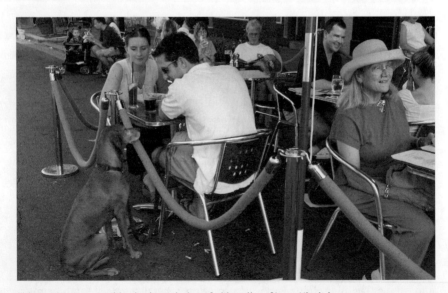

Fidos must stay outside the boundaries of sidewalk cafés at Virginia restaurants.

(Alexandria Convention & Visitors Association)

Sharp Top at the Peaks of Otter, in Virginia's Blue Ridge.

see all that Virginia has to offer in one short trip. Whether you're visiting from out of state or traveling within Virginia, you will want to pick one region to explore at a time. Bordered by West Virginia, Maryland, North Carolina, Tennessee, Kentucky, and, to the east, the Atlantic Ocean, Virginia encompasses 42,769 square miles. Its western and southwestern regions are mountain paradises, while the eastern side of the state is all about the water. Virginia's Piedmont, the largest area, is agricultural and filled with the vineyards, plantations, and historical sites of its forefathers. We've highlighted the most visited attractions in the state, from the mountains to the sea, and tried to provide centrally located accommodation options for each region so that you and Fido can follow your passions.

Today, more than half of US households include a furry family member, and traveling with your best friend has become more widely accepted. Many of the major luxury hotel chains and budget-friendly motel groups welcome pets, but there is a definite difference between "pets allowed" and "pet friendly." While this guide provides as many choices and pet-travel resources as possible, the focus is on accommodations and attractions that go the extra mile for Fido and family.

At the beginning of each chapter, you'll find the Fido 411, Travel 411, and D-Tails: a quick reference guide of local resources for pet services, as well as travel information for the region. This is meant to be a timesaver, but by no means is it a replacement for the local yellow pages or the detailed listings in each region's chapter.

You'll also see that we've highlighted some of the best things to do with your four-legged friend in our Tail Wagger feature and have pointed out some must-see attractions and restaurants that are worth the cost of a pet sitter or daycare.

Virginia State Parks

The Commonwealth of Virginia has 35 parks across the state, giving visitors a chance to explore hardwood forests, coastal marshes, and flowering meadows. Offering access to the four largest lakes in the state, as well as the Atlantic Ocean and Chesapeake Bay, some parks also have lakes stocked with bass, trout, crappie, and bream for anglers to pursue (a Virginia fishing license is required). There are beaches and pools at 16 of the parks, open from Memorial Day Weekend through Labor Day Weekend, and many parks also offer canoe, paddleboat, kayak, and bike rentals. All of Virginia's state parks are pet friendly, and those with campgrounds and cabins also welcome canine overnight guests for a small additional per-night fee. Dogs

must be on a six-foot leash at all times while in the parks, and are not allowed in public buildings, swimming, or concession areas. Park cabins are climate controlled and furnished with everything from dishes to linens, and many have fireplaces or outdoor grills. All parks have picnic areas and grills, with larger parks also offering picnic shelters for rent for large gatherings. With over 500 miles of trails in Virginia state parks, including trails for horseback riding and cycling, self-guided hikes allow visitors to experience both the natural beauty and cultural history of each unique area. Some of

Enjoy boating at Smith Mountain Lake State Park.

Virginia's parks were built by the Civilian Conservation Corps (CCC), and Pocahontas State Park outside Richmond is home to the CCC Museum. Many parks also feature restored historic buildings that are open to the public, from an antebellum mansion at Chippokes Plantation State Park along the James River to a 19th-century farmhouse at Sky Meadows, on the eastern side of the Blue Ridge Mountains. Leesylvania, Sailor's Creek Battlefield, and Staunton River Battlefield offer Civil War living-history programs, while Wilderness Road State Park in the far western reaches of the state relives Virginia's frontier heritage. The most visited park in Virginia, First Landing State Park in Virginia Beach, was the site of the European settlers' first footsteps in the New World, although a skirmish with Native Americans convinced them to reboard their ships and look for a safer location, at Jamestown.

To take a virtual tour of Virginia's state park trails, visit www.virginiaout doors.com or, for more information on specific state parks, see www.dcr .virginia.gov/state_parks

The Sheraton Roanoke provides comfy beds and bowls for visiting Fidos.

(Courtesy of the Sheraton Roanoke)

Where to Stay

First and foremost, while we strive to provide up-to-date information on rates and pet policies, these can change in an instant, so always call to confirm both before booking. Since pet-friendly rooms are limited at many hotels, most require an advance reservation, although midrange and budget hotels along major highways welcome walk-ins. Some hotels have weight or breed restrictions, some charge a cleaning fee or an additional fee per night or per pet, and most require proof of vaccination and flea treatments. The rules and rates vary by property, as well as by season, and often these details are not covered in full on the company website, which is why you must call and speak to a real human.

In general, hotels in the luxury category are the most pet-centric. Loews Hotels have a Loews Loves Pets program with tons of amenities for both you and Fido. The Waldorf Astoria Collection also has a Very Important Pet program, while Starwood properties feature Love That Dog amenities. Ritz-Carlton, Omni, and Kimpton also cater to dog lovers. Large chains including Hilton and Holiday Inn have recently jumped on the pet-friendly bandwagon as well. Amenities range from special doggy beds, mats, bowls, and treats to doggy spa treatments, onsite pet-sitting and dog-walking services, and special canine room-service menus.

In the moderate and budget range, smaller hotels and motels allow pets but offer few, if any, amenities for their four-legged visitors. Be aware that because many of these properties are franchised, policies may vary.

Hotel Pet Programs and Amenities

In general, hotels can require presentation of vaccination documents and proof of flea treatment at check-in. Many hotels prohibit leaving dogs unattended in rooms, and most require four-legged guests to be crated if left unattended. In most cases, guests must sign a waiver assuming responsibility for any damage caused by the pet, and many hotels will charge a nonrefundable cleaning fee or daily additional fee per pet or per stay. Remember that it's up to the individual hotel's discretion to accept pets over the stated weight limit or if they consider a pet to be dangerous, frightening, or disruptive to other guests, so always call the hotel directly to clarify the details of their pet policy and discuss any concerns. Even if a hotel or motel chain has a corporate pet-friendly policy, there may be properties that are not able to accept pets due to local or state ordinances.

Jake, a Virginia Beach resident, loves to run on the beach.

Here are some of the perks and services you can expect at the industry's pet-centric properties:

Hilton: The Hilton family, which encompasses several brands including DoubleTree, Embassy Suites, Waldorf Astoria, Hampton, and Homewood Suites, offers a "Creature Comforts" pet package of amenities at many of their locations. Included in Fido's room are two dog bowls and a place mat, and at check-in your furry friend will get his or her own welcome gift, which includes organic treats, biodegradable waste bags, a travel tote, and a travel-size bottle of deodorizing disinfectant.

There is a two-pet-per-room limit, a 75-pound weight limit, and a $75 nonrefundable pet fee. You must reserve a pet-friendly room in advance at 1-800-Hiltons or by calling the individual hotel directly.

Kimpton: Kimpton claims "leader of the pack" status as the first full-service hotel company to welcome four-legged visitors. Their "HosPETality" includes not only beds and bowls, but also no additional fees or weight limits, and they even have a Director of Pet Relations (a tail-wagging canine ambassador) at some of their properties. Amenities include pet door hangers, local lists of pet-friendly businesses, and luxury services including doggy massage, gourmet canine cuisine, and pet sitting. All 52 Kimpton properties welcome pets with absolutely no restrictions, and if you can't bring your own, they'll lend you a goldfish through their "Guppy Love" program. Some locations host regular Yappy Hours for their four-legged guests!

Loews: "Loews Loves Pets" is their slogan, and it's true. Amenities range from gifts of pet tags and treats to in-room bowls, mats, and paw-imprinted "Do Not Disturb" door hangers. Various properties offer a wide range of pet services, from doggy massage and pet sitting to canine room service, and guests receive a list of nearby pet services and dog-walking routes. Loews also partners with Banfield Pet Hospitals to offer four-legged guests a complimentary examination and a 15 percent discount on services should a health issue arise during your stay. Loews allows two pets per room and charges a onetime $25 cleaning fee.

Ritz-Carlton: With some exceptions, most Ritz-Carlton properties are super pet-friendly, although specific pet policies like weight limit and number of pets per room may vary, as do the pet amenities and fees. Most hotels charge a onetime cleaning fee ($125–150) and offer pet treats, bowls, mats, and other amenities. Standard weight limits are 25 pounds, but some Ritz-Carltons do allow larger dogs upon request.

Starwood: The Starwood group, which includes Sheraton, Westin, and W Hotels, has the Love That Dog program, which includes a canine version of their signature Heavenly Bed for your pal, in addition to doggy bowls, toys, and treats. Some locations also offer canine massage. The luxury boutique hotels in the W group are all pet friendly, but policies vary at the other brands. Pets up to 40 pounds are allowed at the W Hotels, and up to 80 pounds at some Westin and Sheraton properties. Fees and deposits vary by hotel (at W, expect to pay an extra $25 per day and a nonrefundable $100 cleaning fee), and you may not leave pets unattended in your room.

Pet-iquette

Hotels and attractions that welcome pets do so as an added amenity or privilege for their human customers. You and Fido are guests and expected to behave as such. And since dogs can't read the list of rules, you're responsible for making sure your furry family members are on their best behavior. Here are five rules that are nonnegotiable:

1. Always clean up after your pet. While many dog parks, hotels, and even some rest areas along the interstates have poo-bag dispensers, always carry a supply of your own.

2. Always put Fido in his crate when you will be out of the hotel room. Yes, even if you're only going down to the lobby to ask a question or down the hall to get ice! In fact, many hotels do not allow dogs to be left unattended in rooms even if they are crated, as they may bark or howl if they become distressed, and disturb other guests. Crating your pooch will keep him or her safe . . . what if a housekeeper enters a room where a pet is loose and the pet escapes? If you need to be away from your room for any length of time and can't take your pooch, find out if the hotel offers in-room pet sitting or can refer you to a nearby doggy daycare.

3. Your dog must be on a leash at all times when not in your room. This includes all public areas of the hotel and in any walking situation. Most states and cities have leash laws, so unless you're in a fenced dog park where your friend can run safely, you need to keep him leashed.

Hotels Along the Interstates

If you're driving to Virginia, these are the chains you'll see off most inter-state exits. They are probably your best bets for a quick stopover with your pet.

Best Western www.bestwestern.com/tripplanner/travelwithpets.asp

Candlewood Suites www.candlewoodsuites.com

Choice Hotels www.choicehotels.com/en/pet-friendly-hotels?sid= gPdp.Ib8lhgR2Dg.10 These include:

> Ascend, Clarion, Comfort Inn & Suites, Econo Lodge, Quality Inn & Suites, Mainstay Inn & Suites, Rodeway, Sleep Inn, Suburban

Crowne Plaza www.crowneplaza.com

Doubletree http://doubletree.hilton.com/en/dt/promotions/dt_ petfriendly/index.jhtml?WT.srch=1

Embassy Suites http://embassysuites1.hilton.com/en_US/es/index.do

Hampton Inn http://hamptoninn1.hilton.com/en_US/hp/index.do

Hilton www.hilton.com/en/hi/promotions/hi_pets/index.jhtml

Holiday Inn www.holidayinn.com

Holiday Inn Express www.hiexpress.com

Homewood Suites http://homewoodsuites.hilton.com/en/hw/hotels/hotelpromo.jhtml? ctyhocn=BALHWHW&promo=BALHWHW_Service_pets

Hotel Indigo www.hotelindigo.com

JW Marriott Hotels & Resorts www.marriott.com/pet-friendly-hotels.mi. These include:

> Courtyard by Marriott, Fairfield Inn by Marriott, Marriott Hotels & Resorts, Residence Inn by Marriott, SpringHill Suites by Marriott, TownePlace Suites by Marriott, Renaissance Hotels

La Quinta Inn & Suites www.LQ.com

Motel 6 www.motel6.com

Red Roof Inn www.redroof.com

Staybridge Suites www.StayBridge.com

Studio 6 www.staystudio6.com

NOTE: Not every location of these chains is guaranteed to be pet friendly, so call to check the specific hotel's policies before booking.

4. Don't allow your animals on hotel furniture. The reason many hotels charge a cleaning fee is that loose animals that get on chairs and beds not only get them dirty but can also spread fleas and germs. Even if Fido sleeps in your bed at home, remember that you aren't at home! If your pooch doesn't like sleeping in his crate, bring a dog bed along.

5. Don't take Fido to public attractions unless he or she is well behaved. Incessant barking, begging, or canine shenanigans can ruin the experience for other visitors.

Virginia Do's and Don'ts

Virginia welcomes canine visitors in both national and state parks, with some restrictions. Dogs must be on a six-foot leash and are not allowed in concession areas or in public buildings, and of course, humans are expected to clean up after their four-legged friends. At state parks, canines can camp or stay in cabins with their humans for an additional fee (not all parks offer overnight accommodations) and Virginia's premier national park, Shenandoah, welcomes dogs in their lodges.

Since most of Virginia is heavily wooded, especially the park areas, you'll need to check yourself and your pal often for ticks. Virginia has four types of ticks: the lone star tick, the American dog tick, the brown tick, and the deer tick. Both the lone star and American dog tick are potential carriers of Rocky Mountain spotted fever. Small tick larvae, called "seed ticks," are difficult to spot: on a human they look like a freckle, and on a dog, like a speck of dirt.

Famous Four-Legged Virginians
ALL THE PRESIDENTS' DOGS

Virginia is known as the Mother of Presidents, with eight of the nation's leaders hailing from the Old Dominion. Many of them were dog lovers as well: George Washington was an avid foxhunter and owned a pack of hounds named Mopsy, Taster, Cloe, Tipler, Forester, Captain, Lady Rover, Vulcan, Sweetlips, and Searcher. Renaissance man Thomas Jefferson owned a sheep dog and instituted the first dog license in the state, while James Monroe was a spaniel man. Woodrow Wilson didn't own a dog, but shook hands with one who was a war hero: Stubby, a bull terrier, captured a German spy in World War I.

Five 5-Woof Facts about Virginia

1. Pet-friendly Virginia Beach is the world's largest pleasure beach, with 28 miles of oceanfront.

2. Virginia has 2,500 miles of scenic drives, with lots of pet-friendly stops along the way.

3. Many of Virginia's 200+ wineries welcome pets or have canine ambassadors.

4. Virginia State Parks are consistently voted to be America's best, and welcome leashed pets on trails and in cabins and campgrounds.

5. Virginia's famous Shenandoah National Park offers pet-friendly accommodations at its lodges.

Good manners are an ingrained part of Virginia's social culture, and as long as you and your dog are friendly and well behaved, you'll find a warm welcome throughout the Old Dominion.

Getting to Virginia and Getting Around

Sixty percent of the US population lives within a day's drive or less, so it's no surprise that most visitors to Virginia are traveling by car within the state. If you and Fido are flying to Virginia, there are major airports in every region, but you'll need a rental car to get around unless you're staying in a metropolitan area like Northern Virginia or Richmond. Unfortunately, Fido is not allowed on Amtrak trains, although you may bring a crated pet on the Metrorail subway and Metrobus systems serving the DC metropolitan area.

Flying

Virginia has eight primary airports, with the two largest, Reagan and Dulles, located near Washington, DC:

CHO-Charlottesville Albemarle Airport www.gocho.com

LYH-Lynchburg Regional Airport (Preston Glenn Field) www.lynchburgva.gov/index.aspx?page=85

PHF-Newport News/Williamsburg (Patrick Henry Field) www.flyphf.com

ORF-Norfolk International Airport www.norfolkairport.com

RIC-Richmond International Airport (Byrd Field) www.flyrichmond.com

ROA-Roanoke Regional Airport (Woodrum Field) www.roanokeairport.com

DCA-Ronald Reagan Washington National Airport www.metwash airports.com/reagan

IAD-Washington Dulles International Airport www.metwashairports .com/dulles

Driving

INTERSTATES

Several major interstate highways run through Virginia. I-95 runs north to south for 170 miles to the North Carolina state line, while the other north-to-south highway, I-81, runs from just south of Martinsburg, West Virginia, for 320 miles to the Tennessee state line. I-85 brings travelers from North Carolina to Petersburg, Virginia, while I-77 runs from North Carolina to the southwest part of the state. I-64 runs east to west across the state from the Allegheny Highlands to Hampton Roads, and I-66 connects the northern Shenandoah Valley with Northern Virginia and Washington, DC.

STATE ROADS AND SCENIC DRIVES

Many of Virginia's most scenic drives are along state and US primary routes, designated by black-and-white signs with a shield emblem. Some routes, like US 1 and US 11, run parallel to I-95 and I-81, so you can easily go from one to the other. Historical attractions are often on these routes: for example, Natural Bridge is on US Route 11 (also known as Lee Highway), while US Route 250 runs east-west near I-64 through the cities of Charlottesville and Richmond, becoming Broad Street in the capital city.

The most confusing parts of the highway system are the myriad connec-

Fido Frequent-Flier Miles

Two of the pet-friendly airlines that fly into Virginia's major airports offer frequent-flier points for your pooch. Sign up for **JetBlue Airway's JetPaws** program (www.jetblue.com/flying-on-jetblue/pets/about.asp) and you'll get an extra 300 True Blue points, a special tag for your pet carrier, a list of pet-iquette tips, and a complimentary pet-travel guide to JetBlue destinations. **Virgin Atlantic's Flying Paws** (www.virgin-atlantic.com/en/gb /frequentflyer/fcnewsfeatures/nf_flying_paws.jsp) gives humans 1,000 Flying Club miles each time their pet travels, and Fido gets a "Welcome Onboard Pet Pack" on his "virgin" flight.

tors and beltways. These always begin with a 2, 3, 4, or 5: for example, I-264 runs for 13 miles through Chesapeake, Portsmouth, and Norfolk, while I-464 is a 6-mile connector to Virginia Beach. The Capital Beltway, I-495, and the many connectors in and around Northern Virginia and Washington, DC, can be especially difficult to navigate.

Virginia has fewer than 10 toll roads, with most located in Northern Virginia, central Virginia, and Hampton Roads. Many of these are short crosstown routes, like the Powhite Parkway and Downtown Expressway in Richmond. Rates vary from 25 cents to the $12 fee for passenger vehicles on the famous Chesapeake Bay Bridge-Tunnel. E-ZPass (www.ezpassva.com) is accepted at most locations, including the Bridge-Tunnel.

Driving through the mountains provides spectacular scenery like this waterfall near Clifton Forge.

While Virginia residents may groan about paying the state income tax and personal property taxes, those funds have created and maintained some of the best scenic highways and parks in America, as well as a vast network of visitor centers and rest areas.

SPECIAL CONSIDERATIONS

Roads through the mountains can be hazardous in rain, fog, and snow, and there are often winter weather closures on Skyline Drive and the Blue Ridge Parkway. In the summer, be on the lookout for white-tailed deer and other wildlife, and in fall, for heavy traffic from local and visiting leaf-peepers. Keep your gas tank topped off while driving through the mountains, as gas stations are scarce along many routes.

If you're heading to Virginia Beach, the Eastern Shore, the Northern Neck, or one of the many lakes or river resorts in the state, traffic on Fridays

Driving 411

The **Virginia Department of Transportation** (www.virginiadot .org) is an invaluable resource for driving through the state, with extensive information on the highway system, welcome centers and rest areas, road closures, and travel distances.

and Sundays can be backed up for miles. The Chesapeake Bay Bridge-Tunnel can also get backed up during rush hours and on weekends as locals escape to the shore.

Speed limits vary, even changing along the interstates, so be sure to check the road signs for the posted limit. On scenic drives, like Skyline Drive and the Blue Ridge Parkway, speed limits are low (35 or 45 MPH) due to the curvy mountain roads and abundant wildlife. On many maps, mile markers are used in lieu of exit numbers, and they are used exclusively on the scenic Skyline Drive and Blue Ridge Parkway to define a location. These are usually noted as "MM" preceding the mile numeral (for example, MM120).

Welcome Centers and Rest Areas

Virginia's 12 Welcome Centers are open and staffed seven days a week from 8:30 A.M. to 5 P.M.

Clear Brook Welcome Center, I-81S at VA/WV line (540-722-3448)

Fredericksburg Welcome Center I-95S at MM131 (540-786-8344)

New Church Welcome Center US 13 at MD state line (757-824-5000)

Skippers Welcome Center, I-95N at VA/NC Line (434-634-4113)

Bracey Welcome Center I-85N at NC/VA line (434-689-2295)

Lambsburg Welcome Center at Lambsburg I-77N (276-755-3931)

Bristol Welcome Center I-81N at TN state line (276-466-2932)

Rocky Gap Welcome Center I-77 (276-928-1873)

Virginia's rest areas feature pet-walking areas, but your friend must remain on a leash at all times.

Most of Virginia's rest stops have picnic tables so you and your pal can share lunch.

Covington Welcome Center I-64 East (540-559-3010)

Bell Tower Visitor Center on Capitol Square in Richmond (804-545-5584)

East Coast Gateway Welcome Center, I-64E, MM213 (804-966-7450)

Manassas Welcome Center, I66 West (703-361-2134)

Welcome centers and safety rest areas along the interstate highways have designated pet-walking areas, and many have doggy cleanup stations, but always carry a supply of cleanup bags for those that don't. Many of the rest areas also have sheltered picnic areas if you want to take a break for lunch.

Fido's Packing List

Here's a checklist of must-haves to pack for your pooch.

1. Current vaccination and flea-treatment records, and paper copies of any prescription medication if you can't refill it before you leave. It's a good idea to have your regular vet just make a copy of all records in case you have any medical problems on the road, especially if your dog has a preexisting condition or is a senior.

2. A portable crate for car travel and hotel stays.

3. A supply of drinking water and pet food.

4. Food and water bowls (not all hotels supply these).

5. Paper towels and poo bags for easy cleanup.

6. Collar with ID and rabies tags and a sturdy leash.

Top Civil War Sights in Virginia

More battles were fought in Virginia than in any other state during the Civil War, and during the multiyear Sesquicentennial Celebration, Virginia will host many special events and exhibits about the conflict and its impact on the nation. Key sites for history buffs include:

Appomattox Court House National Historical Park (www.nps.gov/apco)

Fredericksburg & Spotsylvania National Military Park (www.nps .gov/frsp)

Manassas National Battlefield Park (www.nps.gov/mana)

New Market Battlefield State Historical Park (www.4.mi.edu/museum /nm/)

Pamplin Historical Park & The National Museum of the Civil War Soldier (www.pamplinpark.org)

Petersburg National Battlefield (www.nps.gov/pete)

Richmond National Battlefield Park (www.nps.gov/rich)

Virginia Civil War Trails (www.civilwartraveler/EAST/VA/)

7. A current photo (if for some reason you lose your pet, you'll need a photo for flyers and online postings).

8. Favorite toys, blankies, or dog bed.

If You Lose Your Pet

It happens more often than you might think . . . a vacation turns into a tragedy because a beloved pet gets lost. This often happens when pets that are allowed to travel "loose" in a car dart out at a rest area or pit stop. Keeping your pet in a crate in the car, and with a collar on at all times, is the safe way to travel. Likewise, if your pet is loose in a strange hotel room and a service person comes into the room, the animal is likely to flee, so if you must leave your dog unattended, put it in its crate even if you're only leaving for a few minutes.

If the worst happens and your pooch does get lost, immediately search the area. If you still can't find your dog, you'll need to:

1. Create a flyer with a current photo and your contact information and post it in and around the area where your pup escaped.

2. Post ads on Craigslist for the area you were in when the pooch got lost and any nearby towns.

3. Call the local newspaper and place a "Lost Pet" classified ad. In many towns, these are free.

4. Call all the local animal shelters and veterinarians to see if an animal matching the description of your pet has been turned in. Again, having a current photo for this is a must!

5. If your animal is microchipped or registered with a pet-finder website, check those sources. It's important to make sure you keep your contact information up to date with these services.

6. Don't give up! It can sometimes take several days for a lost pet to be dropped off at a shelter or for your ads and notices to be posted.

Travel with Pets—Additional Resources

Every search engine on every website has its own database, and none of them includes every single pet-friendly accommodation or service, so you should check several of the top sites to see which hotels or pet-friendly attractions appear in several places. Some are better for information, some for maps and routes, some for accommodations, and some for leisure activities. Also, some websites list only advertisers, and while many of those may be perfectly good choices for you and your pet, it's a skewed look at what's available. Most of the sites link directly to the source, whether it's a hotel, airline, or pet store, and it's always a good idea to follow up by phone as information and policies can change overnight. Here are some of our favorite pet-travel resources to help plan your trip:

Virginia Tourism Corporation
www.virginia.org
Enter "pet friendly" in the search box on the home page and you'll get close to 1,000 results for accommodations, attractions, and special events that welcome four-legged visitors. Virginia is truly for dog lovers!

Fido Friendly
www.fidofriendly.com
www.fidofriendlyapartments.com
One of the first national travel magazines devoted to traveling with dogs, *Fido Friendly*'s motto is "Leave no dog behind," and to that end, the magazine is full of in-depth features on pet-friendly accommodations and destinations, as well as reviews of pet-travel products. The website has a search engine for several pet-friendly categories, and there is a separate

Virginia National Parks

Most of Virginia's national parks and historic sites operated by the National Park Service are pet friendly, with the exception of Assateague Island National Seashore, where environmental concerns exclude four-legged visitors on the Virginia side of the island. Dogs must be on a six-foot leash at all times and are not allowed in public buildings, near concession or swimming areas, or on some restricted trails. Fees vary by park, with senior, student, and military discounts available, and all parks honor the National Parks and Federal Recreational Lands annual pass (www.nps.gov/finda park/passes.htm).

There are several days a year when the parks offer free admission:

January 14–16 Martin Luther King Jr. Weekend

April 21–29 National Park Week

June 9 Get Outdoors Day

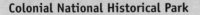

September 29 National Public Lands Day

November 10–12 Veterans Day Weekend

www.nps.gov/findapark/feefreeparks bystate.htm

Appomattox Court House National Historical Park

www.nps.gov/apco/index.htm

On Palm Sunday in 1865, General Robert E. Lee surrendered at Appomattox Court House, ending what Virginians refer to as the War Between the States.

The main lodge at Big Meadows in Shenandoah National Park.

Colonial National Historical Park

www.nps.gov/colo/index.htm

Colonial America began in 1607 with the first permanent settlement at Jamestown, and ended at Yorktown with the final major battle of the American Revolutionary War. A 24-mile scenic, Colonial-style parkway connects Colonial Williamsburg, Jamestown, and Yorktown to create what is known as Colonial National Historical Park. Stroll through the original fort at Jamestown, where archaeologists are still unearthing American history, or walk along the waterfront in charming Yorktown.

George Washington Memorial Parkway's Great Falls Park

www.nps.gov/grfa/index.htm

The 800-acre Great Falls Park is centered around the falls where the Potomac River descends over the steep rocks to Mather Gorge, and offers numerous hiking trails and recreational opportunities. The park is just one of the highlights along the George Washington Memorial Parkway.

Manassas National Battlefield Park

www.nps.gov/mana/index.htm

Two major battles of the Civil War, one in 1861 and another in 1862, were fought on the fields overlooking Bull Run.

Petersburg National Battlefield

www.nps.gov/pete/index.htm

Canines in cars are welcome to accompany their humans on a driving tour of the grounds, or on foot, but aren't allowed in the visitor center.

Prince William Forest Park

www.nps.gov/prwi/index.htm

With 37 miles of hiking trails that meander through a 15,000-acre piedmont forest, Prince William Forest Park welcomes furry friends and even hosts a Paws in the Park Day every summer, with special demonstrations like Top Doggy Chefs and canine massages.

Shenandoah National Park

www.nps.gov/shen/index.htm

One of the most popular national parks in America, Shenandoah National Park has more than 500 miles of trails, as well as pet-friendly accommodations in the lodges at Big Meadows and Skyland. The park's scenic Skyline Drive is one of the most beautiful drives in the country, with more than 75 overlooks along the way.

website for pet-friendly rentals. The FF Travel Club Membership is a good value ($35 for one year, $45 for two) offering a subscription to the magazine, membership in 1-800-HELP-4-PETS, and a variety of discounts at participating hotels and pet retailers.

Pets on the Go

www.petsonthego.com

What we like about this site is that it is written and compiled by professional journalists. There are several excellent destination reviews, but you

Wining (and Woofing) Your Way through Virginia

With more than 200 wineries in nine regions and six American Viticultural Areas (AVAs), Virginia is the fifth-largest producer in America, and in 2012 was named as one the world's Top 10 Wine Destinations by *Wine Enthusiast* magazine. Throughout the state, you can taste Virginia's vintages, with terroir from the Atlantic Coast to the Blue Ridge Mountains. Most of Virginia's vineyards and wineries that are open to the public also welcome four-legged visitors, and several host special events for canines or feature pet-friendly accommodations and amenities. Virginia's wine trails are designed on popular routes that also highlight the state's natural beauty and historic attractions: signs featuring clusters of grapes mark the trails and point the way to vineyards. Detailed information on Virginia's wine regions, AVAs, trails, and wineries is available at the website Virginia Wine, www.virginiawine.org.

Virginia is for wine lovers.

Artisanal Wineries of Rappahannock County www.artwinerc.com

Bedford County Wine Trail www.bedfordwinetrail.com

Blue Ridge Wine Trail www.blueridgewinetrail.com

Blue Ridge Wine Way www.blueridgewineway.com

must be a subscriber to view a lot of the detailed content on activities. They also offer a travel club membership similar to Fido Friendly's.

PetTravel.com

www.pettravel.com

This is a great website for detailed travel information including airline and car-rental pet policies, information on what kind of veterinary certificate you need, and even immigration rules and forms for international travel. It has a database of more than 31,000 listings.

Pets Welcome

www.petswelcome.com

The best feature on this website is a search function that allows you to put in the address you're departing from and the address you're going to and get not only a map but also a list of pet-friendly accommodations on

Blue Ridge "Whiskey Wine Loop" www.discovershenandoah.com /whiskey-wine-loop/

Botetourt County Wine Trail www.botetourtwinetrail.com

Chesapeake Bay Wine Trail www.chesapeakebaywinetrail.com

Colonial Virginia Wine Trail www.ColonialVirginiaWineTrail.com

Eastern Shore Wine Trail www.esvatourism.org

Explore Nelson Wine Trail www.nelsoncounty.com/visit/wineries brewery/

Fauquier County Wine Trail www.fauquiertourism.com/wineries.html

Foothills Scenic Wine Trail www.FootHillsScenicWineTrail.com

The General's Wine and History Trail www.thegeneralswinetrail.com

Heart of Virginia Wine Trail www.hovawinetrail.com

Jefferson Heritage Trail www.jeffersonheritagetrail.com

Loudoun Wine Trail www.visitloudon.org

Monticello Wine Trail www.monticellowinetrail.com

Mountain Road Wine Experience www.mountainroadwineexperience .com/

Nelson 151 www.nelson151.com/

Shenandoah County Wine Trail www.ShenandoahTravel.org

Shenandoah Valley Wine Trail www.svwga.org

Southern Virginia Wine Trail www.sovawinetrail.com

Tuskie's Wine Trail www.tuskies.com/WineTrail/

Vintage Piedmont www.vintagepiedmont.com/

your route with specifics like phone numbers, pet policies, and number of miles off the interstate exit. As always, call to check the policies and details. This is like a pet-friendly version of MapQuest . . . maybe they should call it PetQuest!

Trips with Pets

www.tripswithpets.com

The header on this site is "Trips for pets and their people," and it is pet-centric. Two unique features are the list of state leash laws and animal hospitals accredited by the American Animal Hospital Association. The trip planner maps your route with the closest AAHA animal hospitals along the way. This is especially good for people traveling with senior pets or pets with chronic illnesses.

Virginia Beach:
Live the Coastal Canine Life

Virginia is all about LOVE, and what's not to love about the world's largest pleasure beach, especially when that beach loves its four-legged visitors? Virginia Beach offers 28 miles of oceanfront fun for you and your pooch, as well as a 3-mile-long boardwalk perfect for morning and evening strolls. For a break from the sun and surf and just north of the public beach, First Landing State Park offers miles of wooded trails for you and your pal to explore, as well as pet-friendly camping and cabin accommodations. The most visited park in the state, First Landing is located on Cape Henry, where the Virginia Company landed in 1607 before heading to Jamestown to establish

(Continued on page 39)

Jake loves to swim at Virginia Beach, but he knows he shouldn't drink the saltwater.

Fido 411

Here are some of the most important numbers to have when you arrive in Virginia Beach:

✚ 24-hour Emergency Veterinarians

Bay Beach Veterinary Hospital, 4340 Virginia Beach Boulevard (757-340-3913; http://baybeachvets.com). This full-service animal clinic also has emergency after-hours staff on duty 5 P.M. to 8 A.M. weekdays and 24/7 on weekends.

Beach Veterinary Referral Center, 1124 Lynnhaven Parkway (757-468-4900; www.affiliatedanimalcare.com). This 24-hour-a-day, 365-day-a-year emergency facility is directed by Dr. Ben O'Kelley, the only board-certified veterinary emergency and critical-care specialist in the Hampton Roads area. Dr. O'Kelley also directs the Greenbrier Veterinary Referral Service in Chesapeake (757-366-9000).

Blue Pearl Veterinary Partners (formerly Tidewater Animal Emergency & Referral Center), 364 South Independence Boulevard (757-499-5463; http://virginia.bluepearlvet.com). Blue Pearl does not offer primary care, but solely exists to handle emergencies and specialist care for illnesses and injuries that most family veterinarians are not equipped to treat. Skilled veterinarians with advanced training are on duty 24 hours a day to handle tough medical and surgical issues.

Animal Poison Control Center—ASPCA (888-426-4435; www.aspca .org/pet-care/poison-control/). If you think your pet may have ingested a poisonous substance or animal, help is available 24 hours a day, 365 days a year.

To find an emergency-care veterinarian from your smartphone, check the following websites for the closest location:

www.vetsnearyou.com, www.localvets.com, or **www.animalclinics nearyou.com** Enter the zip code of your location and it will bring up a list and map of the closest veterinarians.

24-hour Pharmacies

To find a 24-hour pharmacy, check the store-locator search on one of these websites:

CVS: www.cvs.com

Walgreens: www.walgreens.com

RX List: www.rxlist.com/pharmacy/local_locations_pharmacies.htm

D-Tails

Virginia Beach CVB www.visitvirginiabeach.com

In addition to a sort function for pet-friendly accommodations, you'll find excellent travel information and directions, as well as details on special events and attractions.

First Landing State Park www.first-landing-state-park.org

Get the 411 on camping and cabins, as well as recreational opportunities for you and your furry friend.

Travel 411

Don't let your pooch drink saltwater, and be sure to rinse your pet thoroughly after an outing in the ocean or bay. Also, from Memorial Day to Labor Day, pets are not allowed in the resort beach area, but are permitted in areas north and south of that strip.

the first permanent settlement in the New World.

Pet-friendly accommodations include oceanfront hotels and motels in every price range, and private cottage rentals, in addition to the camping and cabin options at the park. The north end of the beach tends to be more laid-back and less crowded than the main resort strip during high season, and Fido is allowed on the beach north of 42nd Street, while there are restricted areas in the resort strip. The 34-foot statue of King Neptune marks the entrance to Neptune Festival Park at 31st Street, and from Memorial Day to Labor Day you can catch street performances on Beach Street USA (along Atlantic Avenue between 17th and 25th Streets). Dogs are

Beach Safety Tips

It can't be said often enough: even if it feels cool, the sun is deceptive. Your dog can easily get heatstroke or die, if you don't pay attention:

- Stay in the shade whenever possible.
- Give your dog plenty of water often.
- Do not let your dog drink seawater.
- Dogs can sunburn just like humans. Use sun block on his ears, nose, and any thin spots in his coat.
- Avoid walking on asphalt, pavement, and even sand when it's hot: all three can burn your dog's paws.
- Always wash your dog after a swim in saltwater.
- Some dogs can't swim and some dogs don't like being in the water. Don't force your pooch to paddle and NEVER throw a dog into the water.
- Never leave your dog unattended in the water, and watch out for strong tides and rip currents.
- Just like humans, dogs tire faster in the water while swimming, so don't overdo it.

Dogs can enjoy the resort strip of Virginia Beach before 10 A.M. and after 6 P.M. most of the year.

allowed on Virginia Beach before 10 A.M. and after 6 P.M. from the day after Labor Day until Memorial Day, and leashed pets are allowed on the boardwalk at any time of day or night during this time period. Because the resort beach area and boardwalk are extremely crowded during the summer, dogs are not allowed on the boardwalk (filled with cyclists and pedestrians) or on the resort strip of beach from 2nd Street to 42nd Street from Memorial Day to Labor Day.

Expect large crowds during the summer season, from May through early September, and waiting lines at local attractions and restaurants. Traffic to and from the beach is especially heavy on Friday and Sunday afternoons and evenings as Virginia residents take their weekend breaks. The beach can also be crowded during some of its most popular annual events, including the Neptune Festival, the Boardwalk Art Show, the East Coast Surfing Championship, and the Rock & Roll Half Marathon.

For a mouthwatering excursion for both you and Fido, visit the Virginia

Local Virginia Beach resident, Lizzie, shops frequently at the Famers Market.

Famous Four-Legged Virginians

BROWNIES TO BARK ABOUT

Jake, a Virginia Beach resident, loves his morning and evening runs on the beach. His human, Deborah, doesn't mind rinsing the sand and salt off him after he swims and digs his paws into the sand. In fact, she's often inspired by her canine family: the owner of Tokies All Natural and Gluten Free Baking Mixes even named one of her scrumptious brownie mixes, Xanders, after a member of her furry family, and donates a portion of her proceeds to her favorite animal charities.

Jake's human, Deborah, doesn't mind if he gets a little sandy on Virginia Beach.

Beach Farmers Market (open daily) to pick up locally grown produce, enjoy a homemade ice cream cone, or treat your buddy to a delicious dog bone from the butcher shop. For an outdoor adventure of a different sort and to socialize with local four-legged residents, Mount Trashmore is a one-of-a-kind park created from an urban landfill.

Getting to Virginia Beach

While there are several routes to and from the beach, take the Chesapeake Bay Bridge-Tunnel at least once during your trip. Named one of the seven engineering wonders of the modern world, the Bay Bridge-Tunnel stocks a special treat for visiting Fidos. From the north or south, take US 13 to experience this engineering marvel. You can also skip the tunnel and take I-85, I-95, or US 17 from either direction. From the west, I-64, US 460, and US 58 will lead to the beach, and from northwest of Hampton Roads, I-64 connects to I-664 and over the Monitor-Merrimac Memorial Bridge Tunnel. For those flying with Fido, the closest airports are in Norfolk (ORF) and Newport News/Williamsburg (PHF).

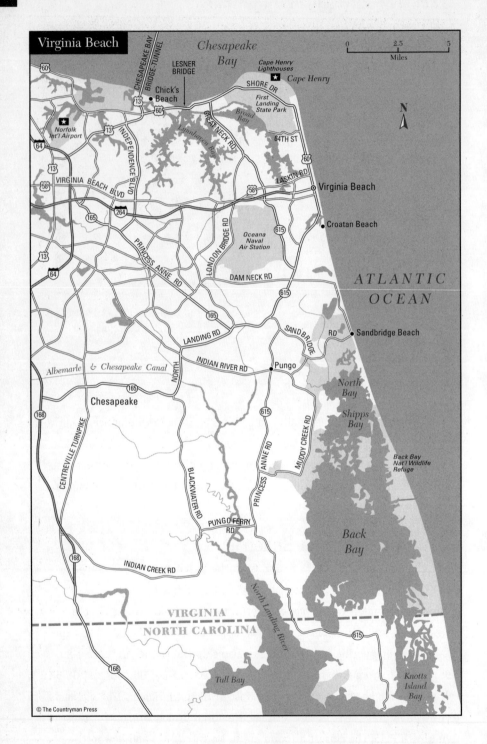

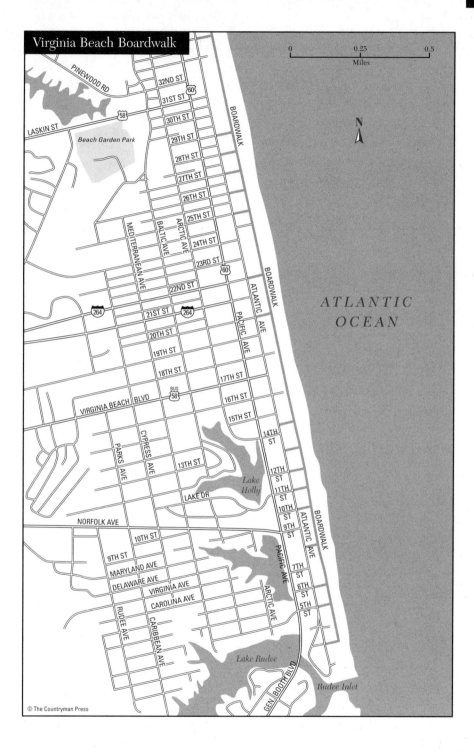

Virginia Beach Boardwalk

ATLANTIC OCEAN

© The Countryman Press

Fido's Favorite Tunnel Treats

One of the seven engineering wonders of the modern world, the Chesapeake Bay Bridge-Tunnel (CBBT) is the largest bridge-tunnel in the world, measuring 17.6 miles from shore to shore, with four artificial islands. The CBBT actually features two tunnels, both a mile long, and two high-level bridges; most of the span is a low-level trestle bridge. At each entrance, toll collectors keep special treats for canines making the crossing: all-natural doggy biscuits shaped like seagulls!

These special treats await dogs crossing the Chesapeake Bay Bridge-Tunnel.

Best Beds: Comfy Sleeps for You and Your Canine Family

Marriott Residence Inn Virginia Beach, 3217 Atlantic Avenue (757-425-1141; www.marriott.com); from $229-379 per night. This is the only pet-friendly extended-stay hotel in the resort beach area. Each suite has a balcony and a full kitchen, as well as separate living and sleeping areas, furnished with natural wicker and serene seaside colors. Added perks include a complimentary hot breakfast and a weekly barbeque. Expect a $100 nonrefundable pet fee per room, but no size or weight limits and up to two pets per room. You must crate your pet in order to receive housekeeping services. You can't take your pooch on this part of the resort beach from Memorial Day to Labor Day, so you'll have to walk north of 42nd Street to get your paws in the sand.

Sheraton Virginia Beach Oceanfront, 3501 Atlantic Avenue (757-425-9000; www.starwood hotels/sheraton); from $300 per night. After a recent multimillion-dollar renovation, the Sheraton Virginia Beach Oceanfront sparkles, with an outdoor pool plaza as well as an indoor pool, a state-of-the-art fitness center, and new suites and rooms with top-shelf amenities, from 37-inch flatscreens to Sheraton's signature Sweet Sleeper beds. The modern lobby features free high-speed Internet access and computer usage. There are no addi-

The Sheraton on Virginia Beach is pet friendly, although pets are prohibited from this stretch of resort beach during the summer.

human guests. The hotel's 244 rooms (166 with oceanfront views) offer free wireless Internet service, MP3/alarm clock, Wolfgang Puck gourmet coffee and tea, and two free bottled waters. Pets up to 60 pounds are welcome with an additional $25-per-day fee.

BEHIND THE BEACH

DoubleTree by Hilton, 1900 Pavilion Drive (757-422-8900; http://doubletree3.hilton.com/en/ hotels/virginia/doubletree-by-hilton-hotel-virginia-beach-ORFB NDT/index.html; from $139 per night. Located six blocks from the ocean and near the convention center, the DoubleTree welcomes pets of all sizes with a $25-per-night additional fee. There's a full-service restaurant in the hotel, and since DoubleTree is a member of the Hilton family, you can use your Honors points for upgrades or free nights.

Founders Inn and Spa, 5641 Indian River Road (757-424-5511; www.foundersinn.com); from $159 per night. This five-star resort with its full-service spa is the farthest from the beach, about 30 minutes from lobby to ocean, but offers complimentary shuttle service. The luxurious Colonial-era décor and lush English gardens are a nod to nearby Colonial Williamsburg, while the stellar conference center and business services speak to the

tional fees for pets, and Sheraton does have loaner pet beds, but you need to reserve one in advance. Dogs up to 90 pounds are allowed, with a two-pet-per-room limit.

Wyndham, 5700 Atlantic Avenue (757-428-7025; www.wyndham .com); from $169 per night. Located north of the resort area, the Wyndham is the only oceanfront hotel where you can take your dog on the beach during the summer months, as access is restricted in the resort beach area, and at this hotel, Fido is considered part of the family. Just walk out the front door and your pooch can romp in the sand before 10 A.M. and after 6 P.M. Each pet-friendly room has a private patio leading to an open lawn, and visiting canines experience the same stellar service as neighboring military bases in Norfolk and Hampton Roads. Pets up to 40 pounds are welcome with a $150 refundable security deposit. Leashed dogs are allowed throughout the resort, and there's also a dedicated pet area.

Westin Town Center, 4535 Commerce Street (757-557-0550; www.starwoodhotels.com/westin/property/overview/index.html?propertyID=1568); from $165 per night. While the Westin is located in the downtown business district of Virginia Beach about a 15-minute drive from the shore, it may be an attractive option if you belong to the Starwood Hotel Group's loyalty program. Canines up to 80 pounds are welcomed with no fees, and you can request a loaner "Heavenly" bed and bowl for your pal when you reserve your room.

Best Bowls: Restaurants Worth a Sitter

Bubba's Seafood Restaurant & Crabhouse, 3323 Shore Drive (757-481-3513; www.bubbasseafoodrestaurant.com). With its weathered wood exterior and waterfront location, Bubba's has a "dock-to-dine" philosophy, with fresh catch delivered daily to its own marina. This is casual coastal dining where the seafood is the star: boat up for lunch or relax on the dockside deck for dinner.

Coastal Grill, 1427 North Great Neck Road (757-496-3348; www.coastalgrill.com). It's a bit hard to find, located a couple of miles inland, but this locally owned gem is said to have the best crabcakes in town. Specials rotate daily, so call ahead to see what's on the menu, and make reservations, as the dining room is usually packed with local foodies.

Eat, 4005 Atlantic Avenue (757-965-2472; www.eatbistro.net). A modern American bistro with an Asian sensibility, Eat features tapas and small plates with a twist on local seafood. Try the blue crab pizza with white truffle oil or the Eastern Shore oyster stew.

Tautog's Restaurant, 205 23rd Street (757-422-0081; www.tautogs.com). Located in a historic 1920s beach cottage (Winston's Cottage), Tautog's owners not only wanted to preserve this slice of oceanfront architectural history, they also wanted to continue a Virginia Beach tradition of casual, coastal dining with an array of regional favorites, from oysters Rockefeller and she-crab soup to sage-and-cornmeal-crusted catfish and crabcakes.

Zoë's Steak & Seafood, 713 19th Street (757-437-3636; www.zoesvb.com). Reservations recommended. Serving only dinner, Zoe's is becoming known on the national food radar, thanks to its James Beard–nominated chef, Jerry Weihbrecht.

Try his famous blue crab mac 'n cheese or clams d'asti, with sausage and scallops in a white wine sauce. The restaurant has an excellent wine list and often holds special wine pairing dinners and tastings.

Tail Waggers: Fido's Favorite Outings

⠿ Dog Parks

Dogs can run off-leash at each of the city's two one-acre dog parks (www.vbgov.com/government/ departments/parks-recreation/ parks-trails/pages/dog-parks.aspx), but there is a $15 registration fee. Both parks are open from 7:30 A.M. to sunset.

Red Wing Metro Park, 1398 General Booth Blvd. (757-437-2038)

Woodstock Community Park, 5709 Providence Rd. (757-366-4538)

⠿ More Tail Waggers

First Landing State Park, 2500 Shore Drive (757-412-2300; www .dcr.virginia.gov/state_parks/fir .shtml); $4 per vehicle weekday and $5 weekend or $10 annual pass; additional fees for parking, fishing, camping. This 2,888-acre park is the most visited in Virginia, and there are plenty of pet-friendly trails to explore. Stroll past the oldest lighthouse in America at Cape Henry (1791) and walk in the footsteps of America's original

colonists, who landed here before settling in Jamestown.

Mount Trashmore, 310 Edwin Drive (757-473-5237; www.virginia beach.com/kids/mount-trashmore); free; open 7:30 A.M. to sunset. You can see this "green volcano" from I-264, towering more than 60 feet in the air. What was once a municipal landfill is now a favorite local park, with two artificial lakes, a mountain trail and perimeter trail, 15 shelters, a full-size basketball court, 4 volleyball courts, and a skateboard center. The park also has a snack center, restrooms, and plenty of parking.

Virginia Beach and Boardwalk
In the slow season (after Labor Day and before Memorial Day), the beach is covered in paw prints as locals and visitors alike romp in the surf or stroll along the 3-mile

In the off-season, Virginia Beach residents often walk their pooches on the boardwalk.

boardwalk. Even in the summer season when Fido is not allowed on the boardwalk or on the resort beach, there's plenty of sand to play in north of 42nd Street.

Virginia Beach Farmers Market, 3640 Dam Neck Road (757-385-4395; www.vbgov.com/farmers market). This daily market has a bounty of fresh local produce, as well as an award-winning bakery, ice cream shop, and a butcher shop that will cut custom-sized dog bones for your pal. Grab a home-made cup or cone from Gilly's Creamery and take home some sweet potato biscuits or tomato pie from Season's Bakery.

The Country Butcher at the Virginia Beach Farmers Market has a freezer full of dog bones.

Virginia Legends Walk, 13th Street Park (www.va-legends.com). Learn about Virginians who have made contributions to the state, the nation, and the world, from tennis great Arthur Ashe and country music queen Patsy Cline to great statesmen like James Monroe.

☺ Sweet Treats and Canine Chic: Where to Shop with your BFF

Care-a-Lot Pet Supply, 1924 Diamond Springs Road (757-457-9431; www.carealotpets.com). This is the flagship retail store for a large, online pet retailer with an extensive catalog of great travel accessories for dogs. Check out the soft, collapsible travel crates, leashes, harnesses, seat belts, and other cool gear or stock up on your pal's favorite foods and treats.

Mrs. Bones Bowtique, 1616 Hilltop W. Shopping Center (757-412-0500; www.mrsbones.com). Create your own custom collar and leash from the more than 500 brocade, tapestry, velvet, tartan, and jacquard woven trims at Mrs. Bones. Your pals can shop too and pick out their own patterns and trims (Scotties always go for the plaids!), or pick out a new comfy bed or designer bowl to take home as a souvenir.

Pet Supplies Plus, 5394 Kempsriver Drive (757-424-8448; www.petsuppliesplus.com). In addi-

Famous Four-Legged Virginians
VIRGINIA BEACH'S CANINE TRAVEL PRO

Pooh Bear is an experienced traveler and knows Virginia Beach inside and out. He loves riding in the car and often explores the city and its attractions with his human, Ron Kuhlman, who happens to be the VP of Tourism Marketing for the Virginia Beach Convention & Visitors Bureau. No wonder Ron is such an expert!

Pooh Bear is an expert on the best attractions in Virginia Beach. (Courtesy of Ron Kuhlman)

tion to carrying everything under the Virginia Beach sun that your pal might need on vacation, the store is also home to the PAWS Clinic (Pet Affordable Wellness) offering Sunday clinics for vaccinations.

◉ Big-Box Stores

Petco www.petco.com, 4540 Princess Anne Road (757-474-1018); 2133 Upton Drive (757-430-0306)

PetSmart www.petsmart.com 3413 Virginia Beach Blvd (757-486-1233); 4421 Virginia Beach Blvd (757-497-1279)

♛ A Day of Beauty: Best Pooch Primping

Paws and Purrs Pet Grooming, 5394 Kempsriver Drive (757-424-2252). The grooming shop is located inside the Pet Supplies Plus store, but is a separate business. You can shop for pet food and accessories while your doggie diva has a day of beauty.

Preppie Pooch, 2684 Virginia Beach Boulevard (757-631-5900; www.preppiepooch.com). This doggy day spa offers à la carte add-ons for the upscale version of a bath and nail trim. Indulge your senior dog with a whirlpool hydrotherapy bath or treat your diva to a blueberry facial scrub.

Two Brothers Self Service Dog Wash, 426 Newtown Road (757-497-9274; www.twobrothersdog wash.com). After a day of frolicking in the sand and saltwater, your pooch will need a good washing. The tubs here are sanitized after every wash, and staff will help you lift your big baby in and out if needed. They also supply rubber aprons and all the things you need to bathe your furry friends.

♥ Play Dates: Doggy Daycare

Bayside Kennels, 5201 Virginia Beach Boulevard (757-499-7697; www.baysidekennels.com). With large indoor and outdoor play areas, and a veterinary hospital right next door, Bayside is a popular choice for both boarding and daycare. They also have a dedicated geriatric area for older pets that may not want to socialize with young pups (overnights from $21 and daycare from $18).

Cosmo's Corner, 505 Central Drive (757-457-7834; www.cosmos corneronline.com). Cosmo's offers cage-free boarding and daycare supervised by a certified trainer. With tons of toys and an agility course, the Fido fun is unlimited. Furnished with dog beds, people beds, sofas, and crates, if your pooch stays overnight, he can sleep exactly like he does at home, and there's an attendant on duty 24/7 (overnight from $35 and daycare from $20).

Holly Ridge Manor Canine Country Club, 2993 Seaboard Road (Motel: 757-426-6100 or Daycare: 757-721-7829; http://hollyridge manor.net); motel rooms from $33 per night. This award-winning pet

motel not only has rooms and suites, it also has a penthouse for visiting pooches. Rooms vary in size and amenities (some with television), but all are climate controlled and have piped-in music. Canine guests are personally escorted to the outdoor play areas and pool, and for an additional fee, can have a homemade breakfast in bed of waffles, pancakes, or bagels with cream cheese. Located on a beautiful 60-acre farm, the daycare center (from $25 per day) features the same great play areas and pool, and both daycare and motel guests can order à la carte "spa" services, from baths to pedicures.

Shipp's Corner Pet Spa, 1515 Drakesmile Road (757-301-6941; www.shippscornerpetspa.com); from $33 per night. Created and owned by a veterinarian, Dr. Margaret Johnson, Shipp's Corner is an 11,000-square-foot, state-of-the-art facility where thoughtful details focus on pet health and safety, as well as luxury. Located on several acres filled with wooded trails for long walks, Shipp's Corner also has a heated, pH-balanced indoor pool that's both fun and therapeutic, a special filtration system, hydrotherapy baths, and raised bedding. Luxury suites are furnished with wrought iron beds and mattresses, as well as pet-cams so you can monitor your pet. Add on a facial or massage from the spa to make your buddy's boarding a relaxing retreat.

Worth a Sitter: Sights to See without Fido

Back Bay National Wildlife Refuge, 4005 Sandpiper Road (757-301-7329; www.fws.gov/backbay); $5 per vehicle or $2 pedestrian/bicycle; open daily during daylight hours. The 9,250-acre refuge encompasses coastline with the dunes, marshes, fields, and woodlands that are typical of barrier islands found along the Atlantic coast. The refuge is a habitat for a large variety of wildlife, from loggerhead turtles to bald eagles, and is a migration point for snow geese and ducks in the fall. Dogs are not allowed in the protected habitats, but this is worth a trip for fans of local flora and fauna.

False Cape State Park, 4001 Sandpiper Road (757-426-7128; www.dcr.virginia.gov/state_parks/fal.shtml). This mile-wide spit of barrier island is only accessible by a trail from Back Bay National Wildlife Refuge or by boat. While dogs are allowed in some areas of the park, the trail is often closed to protect wildlife, and some habitat areas are off-limits as well. If you visit between November and March, take the environmentally friendly beach vehicle, the Terra Gator ($8), with tours on weekends that depart from Little Island City Park.

Historic Villages at Cape Henry, First Landing State Park (757-417-7012; www.firstlandingfoundation.com); $8–15 tours and live performances; hours vary June–August. Learn about the first settlers and the Algonquin natives at the live performance of Chip Fortier's play, *1607: First Landing*, or step back into the past in the living history of the re-created settler's village.

Virginia Aquarium, 717 General Booth Boulevard (757-385-3474; www.VirginiaAquarium.com); $21 or $27 with IMAX. The 800,000-gallon aquarium is impressive, but also offers some unique experiences like the Seal Splash, the only 90-minute program in the United States where you actually get to interact with harbor seals. Other premium experiences include behind-the-scenes tours with the staff and boat trips like the Dolphin Watching cruise.

Virginia Museum of Contemporary Art, 200 Parks Avenue (757-425-0000; www.virginiamoca.org); admission varies with exhibitions. The museum is a noncollecting organization that promotes contemporary art through traveling exhibitions and also organizes the summer Boardwalk Art Show on the beach. Check the website for current educational programs and exhibitions.

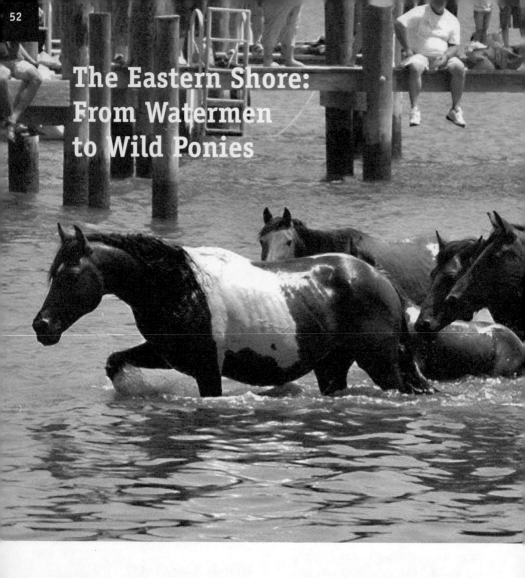

The Eastern Shore:
From Watermen
to Wild Ponies

V irginia's Eastern Shore is a world unto itself, separated from the rest of
the state by the Chesapeake Bay. For over 400 years, farmers have
tilled the flat, fertile land and fishermen have reaped the bounty of oysters,
crabs, and clams from the shallow, tidal flats. Located on the Delmarva
Peninsula, so named because it encompasses parts of three states (Delaware,
Maryland, and Virginia), to the east are the barrier islands, bays, and inlets
that lead to the Atlantic Ocean, and to the west is the Chesapeake Bay.
Nestled at the intersection of the ocean and the bay, the Eastern Shore has
the cleanest water on the coast. Only 70 miles long, the peninsula and its

(Continued on page 55)

Volunteers called "saltwater cowboys" herd the wild ponies during the annual Chincoteague Pony Swim. (Courtesy of the Chincoteague Chamber of Commerce)

Fido 411

Here are some of the most important numbers to have when you arrive in the Eastern Shore:

✚ 24-hour Emergency Veterinarians

Eastern Shore Animal Hospital, 34424 Lankford Hwy, Painter (757-656-4125; www.esanimalhospital.com). This full-service animal clinic has vets on call 24/7. If you have an emergency, call the regular clinic number and follow the instructions to page an on-call veterinarian. This is the only clinic on the Eastern Shore offering after-hours care.

Animal Poison Control Center— ASPCA (888-426-4435 or www .aspca.org/pet-care/poison-control/). If you think your pet may have ingested a poisonous substance or animal, help is available 24 hours a day, 365 days a year.

To find an emergency-care veterinarian from your smartphone, check the following websites for the closest location:

www.vetsnearyou.com, www .localvets.com, or **www.animal clinicsnearyou.com** Enter the zip code of your location and it will bring up a list and map of the closest veterinarians.

Travel 411

Since Virginia's Eastern Shore is a rural region, it's a good idea to bring your own pet foods and medications if you're planning to stay in the area for any length of time. A limited number of pet stores, grooming services, pet sitters, and veterinarians are located in the towns of Onancock, Chincoteague, and Cape Charles.

🌙 24-hour Pharmacies

To find a 24-hour pharmacy, check the store-locator search on one of these websites:

CVS: www.cvs.com

Walgreens: www.walgreens.com

RX List: www.rxlist.com/pharmacy/local_locations_pharmacies.htm

D-Tails

Eastern Shore Tourism www.esvatourism.org

If you're looking for accommodations on the Eastern Shore, the tourism bureau has a pet-friendly sorting function. Just click on Fido's nose to find hotels, motels, B&Bs, or campgrounds that welcome four-legged visitors.

Onancock www.onancock.org

The town of Onancock loves furry visitors and shops proudly display a pet-friendly sticker on their doors. The town's website has a comprehensive pet-friendly section.

Tangier Ferry www.tangierferry.com

Pets are allowed on the ferry to Tangier Island (the only way you can get there) at no additional fee.

The Eastern Shore is known for its fresh oysters, like these from Shooting Point Oyster Company.

islands offer a glimpse into the past. Tangier Island is only accessible by boat, and has its own unique dialect, while, on the Atlantic side, wild ponies still roam the sister islands of Chincoteague and Assateague.

In some ways, not much has changed in this unspoiled region where agriculture and aquaculture are still the primary endeavors. Land trusts protect much of the acreage from developers, and while the residents value their independence and privacy, visitors are warmly welcomed in the small waterfront towns. And although this rural and somewhat rustic region is reminiscent of Virginia life in a simpler century, unspoiled doesn't mean unsophisticated. The towns of Chincoteague, Cape Charles, and Onancock are a mix of historic and hip: 19th-century Victorian homes house modern bed & breakfast inns with Wi-Fi, and eclectic boutiques feature local crafts like stunning sea glass chandeliers and jewelry. Award-winning Chatham Vineyards on Church Creek has a

The boutiques in Cape Charles are a great place to shop for beach cottage chic décor and gift items.

Famous Four-Legged Virginians

ZOE THE THREE-LEGGED DECAF DOG

Kristin and James Willis were tired of the rat race, so they moved to the tranquil Eastern Shore and opened a gourmet coffee roasting business called **Eastern Shore Coastal Roasting** (www.coastal roast.com). Self-avowed "critter lovers," they adopted Zoe from the Eastern Shore SPCA and named their popular decaf coffee after her. Not slowed down a bit by her missing hind leg, Zoe works side by side with her humans every day, and the company makes regular donations to the SPCA in her honor.

Zoe, of Eastern Shore Coastal Roasting Company fame.

canine mascot named Wilbur, who welcomes two- and four-legged guests to their family vineyard in Machipongo. On the other hand, gone, for the most part, are the days when solitary oystermen would gather the sea's bounty in flat-bottomed boats. Today, oysters and clams are cultivated, and the sweet potato and soybean crops leave the region in 18-wheelers rather than wagons. Even outer space now plays a role in the Eastern Shore, with the development of NASA's Wallops Island rocket-launch facility into a major tourist attraction.

You won't find luxury hotel chains or restaurants in this part of Virginia, although there are a few moderately priced motels that welcome pets. Live like a local and sample the casual elegance of the inns, B&Bs, horse farms, and waterfront resorts that offer an abundance of outdoor activities for you and your pooch. Some of the freshest seafood in the state may not be in fine-dining establishments, but in clam shacks and local waterfront eateries along the peninsula. While your choices of dining out with your pooch are limited by the state's health department restrictions, live like a local and have an outdoor picnic with a bushel of crabs, a bucket of steamers, and oysters on the half shell. One of the main tourist attractions that does not allow four-legged visitors is the Chincoteague National Wildlife Refuge: due

Dogs can enjoy the Eastern Shore's rural scene at places like Chatham Vineyards, where Wilbur is the canine greeter.

(Courtesy of Chatham Vineyards)

to environmental concerns, pets are not allowed on this site (not even riding in a car), so you'll need to leave your buddy with a pet sitter or in your lodging. If you're making more than a day trip to the Eastern Shore, be sure to stock up on your pet's food and medications, as you won't find pet stores or veterinarians in many of the towns on the peninsula. Many of the inns and B&Bs offer pet-sitting services, and there is one full-service pet-sitting and dog-walking company based in Cape Charles that has sitters throughout the peninsula. This rural region is not for salon-loving doggy divas, but if your best friend loves the outdoor life, you'll have plenty of opportunities for long strolls or energetic hikes through some of Virginia's most beautiful seaside landscapes.

While dogs are not allowed in the wildlife refuge, the town of Chincoteague is very pet friendly.

(Courtesy ot the Chincoteague Chamber of Commerce)

Famous Four-Legged Virginians

CHINCOTEAGUE'S FAMOUS COOKIES AND THE CANINES WHO INSPIRED THEM

Inge and her two canine companions make all-natural homemade treats at Howl Naturale in Chincoteague. (Courtesy of Howl Naturale)

Ollie and Bumby aren't actually therapy dogs, but when their owner, Inge Veneziano, suffered a neck fracture that forced her to give up her nursing career, it was her two best friends who inspired her to create Howl Naturale. Her goal was to provide all-natural pet treats made with human-grade ingredients (no preservatives, salt, or coloring) to aid in the health and longevity of man's best friend. Howl Naturale became a howling success, with requests for cat treats and equine treats, and Inge also makes the seagull cookies handed out to visiting Fidos at the Chesapeake Bay Bridge-Tunnel. Howl Naturale has been designated as one of Virginia's Finest by the Virginia Department of Agriculture, and Veneziano garnered a Disability Employment Champions Award from the Virginia Department of Rehabilitative Services for her outstanding success. Ollie and Bumby, of course, reap the tasty rewards of success daily, helping their human in the Chincoteague store.

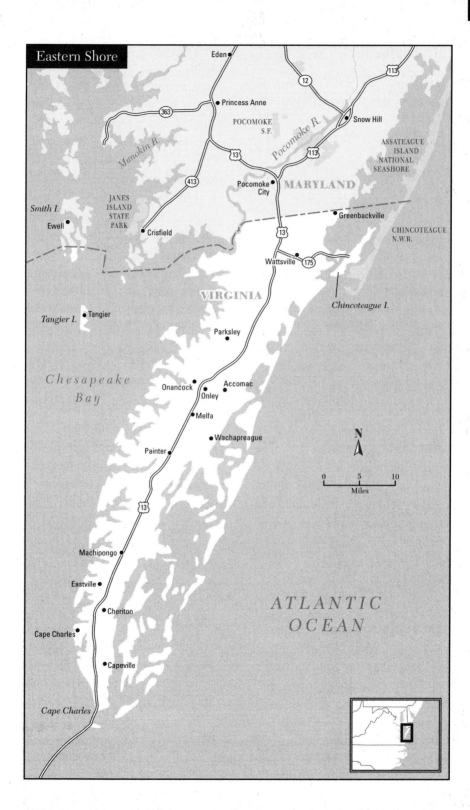

Eastern Shore

Eden

12

113

Princess Anne

363

POCOMOKE
S.F.

Snow Hill

Pocomoke R.

Manokin R.

13

113

ASSATEAGUE
ISLAND
NATIONAL
SEASHORE

413

Pocomoke
City

MARYLAND

Smith I.

JANES
ISLAND
STATE
PARK

Greenbackville

Ewell

Crisfield

CHINCOTEAGUE
N.W.R.

13

Wattsville

175

VIRGINIA

Chincoteague I.

Tangier I. Tangier

Parksley

Chesapeake
Bay

Onancock

Accomac

Onley

Melfa

N

Wachapreague

Painter

0   5   10
Miles

13

ATLANTIC
OCEAN

Machipongo

Eastville

Cheriton

Cape Charles

Capeville

Cape Charles

Best Beds: Comfy Sleeps for You and Your Canine Family

HOTELS & RESORTS

Bay Creek Resort & Club, 500 Marina Village Circle, Route 184/ Stone Road, Cape Charles (757-331-8750; www.baycreekresort.com). Rates vary according to available rentals. With two signature golf courses designed by Jack Nicklaus and Arnold Palmer, and its own marina, beach, restaurants, and shops, Bay Creek offers a limited number of pet-friendly rentals in its Victorian-inspired cottages and condos for a onetime fee of $50 per pet.

Pearce's Waterfront Lodge, 20147 Mosher Lane, Quinby (757-442-7318; www.pearceswaterfrontlodge .com); from $100 per night. Enjoy small-town life in a fishing village and an abundance of outdoor activities at this lodge and collection of cottages on Upshur Bay. Situated on 20 acres, including the historic Quinby Indian burial grounds, there's plenty of room for you and your pal to explore, and you can watch the wild ponies roaming from your window. A $100 refundable pet deposit is required, and pets must be crated when left in the room or cottage.

Sunset Beach Resort Hotel, 32246 Lankford Highway, Cape Charles (757-331-1776; www.sunsetbeach resortVA.com); from $149 per night. Located just north of the Chesapeake Bay Bridge-Tunnel at the tip of the peninsula, the Sunset Beach Resort looks like a throwback to the '60s, with its Jetson-esque round lobby, but has recently been renovated and boasts its own pet-friendly beach and lots of outdoor space for Fido on its 38-acre spread. The 72-room hotel welcomes pets with an additional fee of $15 per day and no weight restrictions, and there's also a pet-friendly RV park on site. Free Wi-Fi and continental breakfast are included in the room rate, and suites have whirlpools, microwaves, and refrigerators.

INNS & B&BS

NOTE: Due to the small size of these establishments, the number of pet-friendly rooms is limited, so book as far in advance as possible.

Channel Bass Inn, 6228 Church Street, Chincoteague Island (757-336-6148; www.channelbassinn .com); from $165–235 per night. It's no surprise that this inn in a late 19th-century house has a tearoom as well, since one of the innkeepers is from England. Surrounded by lush gardens, the inn welcomes well-behaved canines of all sizes with a $10–15 per-night fee, and requests that they be crated in the lovely guestrooms and not allowed on the furniture. The

Famous Four-Legged Virginians

WILBUR THE WINERY HOST

Everyone on the Eastern Shore knows Wilbur, the canine host extraordinaire at Chatham Vineyards. The diminutive dog greets visitors in the parking lot with his tail wagging a mile a minute and leads them to the tasting room door. Often, during the tasting sessions, Wilbur takes a break from his guide duties to relax on the cool floor beneath the wine bar, while guests enjoy Chatham's steel-cut Chardonnay and fresh oysters from the Shooting Point Oyster Company.

Wilbur, the Chatham Vineyards dog, even has an "official" Virginia tourism photo. *Courtesy of Chatham Vineyards)*

room rate includes a gourmet breakfast that includes yogurt parfaits, a variety of pastries, breads, fruit, and cereal, and a hot entrée that changes daily from blueberry pancakes to crab quiche. Musically inclined guests are encouraged to entertain at tea time at what the innkeepers call their Scones & Jam Session, and while the four-course British tea is not included in the room rate, guests get a huge discount, almost half off.

1882 Colonial Manor Inn, 84 Market Street, Onancock (757-787-3521; www.colonialmanorinn.com); from $119 per night. The oldest operating inn on Virginia's Eastern Shore, the Colonial Manor Inn serves a family-style full breakfast and welcomes four-legged guests for an additional $20 per night

(and no weight restrictions) in its two pet-friendly ground-level rooms, which have private access to two acres of parklike grounds. Furry guests are welcomed with treats, pet-sitting services are available, and the innkeeper is certified in pet CPR.

1890's Spinning Wheel Bed & Breakfast, 31 North Street, Onancock (757-787-7311; www .1890spinningwheel.com); from $90 per night. Get a woofer welcome from Molly, the Inn mascot, at this historic Victorian on the Onancock waterfront. Book early, as only one room is pet friendly for dogs under 50 pounds, but the pet fee is a reasonable $10 per night and there is an exclusive fenced play area for your pal. Start your morning with homemade muffins before you and Fido explore the nearby shops and galleries.

Garden and Sea Inn, 4188 Nelson Road, New Church (757-894-9097; www.gardenandseainn.com); $135-205 per night. This romantic Victorian B&B was built in 1802 and was originally known as Bloxom's Tavern. Offering a "Dog Lover's Special Package" that includes a doggy bowl and treats for Fido and chocolates for Fido's human friends, the Garden and Sea Inn has no weight restrictions and a onetime $25-per-pet fee. With a private pool and four beautifully landscaped acres, you'll have plenty of places for long scenic walks with your BFF.

Green Valley Farm Bed & Breakfast, 9929 Bayside Road, Machipongo (757-678-5770; www .greenvalleyfarmbandb.com); from $130 per night. Located on an 85-acre farm, Green Valley welcomes well-behaved dogs and also horses. The farm has its own set of canine kennels, but crate-trained dogs are allowed to stay in rooms and there are no additional fees. Surrounded by four-season gardens and horse pastures, Green Valley has over 20 miles of trails for hiking and horseback riding, and offers cooking classes, as well as kayak and winery tours. The 1800s-era farmhouse is casual and comfortable, and the room rate includes a full breakfast.

Windrush Holidays, 5350 Willow Oak Road, Eastville (757-678-7725; www.windrushholidays.com); from $85 per night. All four-legged visitors are welcome at this spacious horse farm, with a nominal $10-per-day pet fee for canines and $15 per day for equine guests. The restored mid-19th century home houses the bed & breakfast, and a private cottage on the Chesapeake Bay's Smith Beach is also available for rental.

Best Bowls: Restaurants Worth a Sitter

Aqua, 900 Marina Villages Circle, Cape Charles (757-331-8660; www .baycreekresort.com/dining/aqua .asp). Located in the Bay Creek Resort community overlooking the Chesapeake Bay, Aqua has become one of the Eastern Shore's top fine-dining destinations. With a hip lounge area accented with its signature color and a menu that specializes in local seafood and Southern comfort food, this upscale eatery serves both lunch and dinner. Try the local oysters and clams as an appetizer, and then dig into some panko-Parmesan-crusted local flounder or Southern-fried chicken with mashed potatoes.

Bill's Seafood Restaurant, 4040 Main Street, Chincoteague Island (757-336-5831; www.billsseafood

Shack Attack

To truly experience the Eastern Shore lifestyle, pull over for a messy, and incredibly satisfying, lunch or dinner at one of the numerous clam and seafood shacks. Forget the linen tablecloths and candlelight: this is down-and-dirty dining on paper-covered picnic tables, where eating with your hands is considered good manners. Dig in to a bushel of steamers with drawn butter or grab a nutcracker and discover what fresh crab is really all about.

Great Machipongo Clam Shack, 6468 Lankford Highway, Nassawadox (757-442-3800; www.thegreatmachipongoclamshack.com). Dine inside or outside on the picnic tables at this local shack, located on the main north-south Eastern Shore highway. They do have a drive-through as well, if you really can't make the time to stop in, but you'll be missing a quintessential casual seafood experience.

Mallard's at the Wharf, 2 Market Street, Onancock (757-787-8558; www.mallardsllc.com). Everything's historic in the quaint waterfront town of Onancock and that includes Mallard's, located in the old Hopkins Brothers store. Dine on the waterside deck and catch a spectacular sunset, and be sure to ask to meet the musical chef, Johnny Mo.

The Shanty, Cape Charles Harbor, Cape Charles (757-695-3853; www .esvatourism.org/es_where_to_eat). The newcomer to the old-time seafood-shack scene, The Shanty is a favorite for boat-up meals with its prime location on Cape Charles Harbor (dockspace is free for diners), but you're also invited to arrive by golf cart, spaceship, or more traditional means.

For more options, visit the Eastern Shore Tourism website at www.esva tourism.org

restaurant.com). With hand-cut steaks and chops, pasta, and fresh local seafood, Bill's has been a favorite on Chincoteague with locals and pony-loving visitors for more than 50 years. Think classic surf-and-turf favorites from lobster tails and crab imperial to mouthwatering prime rib.

Charlotte Hotel & Restaurant, 7 North Street, Onancock (757-787-7400; www.thecharlottehotel.com). The charming restaurant in this historic boutique hotel in Onancock is where Eastern Shore residents celebrate special occasions. The menu changes frequently as Chef Sam Yokum takes great pride in sourcing ingredients from local watermen and farmers. You'll find something to please every palate with selections that include a meat,

Famous Four-Legged Virginians

BLUE CRAB BAY'S COMPUTER-LITERATE LABRADOODLE

With her own Facebook page, Shiloh the Labradoodle is a local legend on the Eastern Shore, as is her human mom, Pam Barefoot, who built the thriving Blue Crab Bay Company (www.baybeyond.net) from the seafood spice mixes she created on her kitchen table. Named Virginia's Small Business Person of the Year in 1999 and one of the nation's Outstanding Women Entrepreneurs by the US Small Business Administration in 2003, Pam's company now showcases a full line of Eastern Shore products, from her original seasoning mixes to beautiful stoneware designed by Eastern Shore pottery artist José Davis. Shiloh helps her mom at the retail store and with Internet orders, selling popular items like Sting Ray Bloody Mary Mixer, and spicy, honey mustard Virginia Peanuts called Surf Doggies.

Shiloh often works with her mom, Pam, at the Blue Crab Bay Company.

(Courtesy of Blue Crab Bay)

fish, fowl, or vegetarian option. Soft-shell crabs and crabcakes fly out of the kitchen in-season, while vegetarians enjoy the local eggplant braciole. You can also enjoy breakfast here, but dinner is worth the wait.

Island House Restaurant, 17 Atlantic Avenue, Wachapreague (757-787-4242; www.wachapreague .com). Since this iconic restaurant is located at Captain Zed's Marina, where the regional fishing tournaments gather, you can be certain you'll get some of the Eastern Shore's freshest catch. The ambience may be island-casual, but the chef here trained at Johnson & Wales, so you can expect some sophisticated seafood. (The restaurant usually closes for the entire month of January.)

Sting-Ray's, 26507 Lankford Highway, Cape Charles (757-331-1541; www.sting-raysrestaurant .com). A restaurant in an Exxon station? You're at Sting-Ray's, one of the most popular dining destinations on the Eastern Shore for half a century. Located on US 13, about

5 miles north of the Chesapeake Bay Bridge-Tunnel, Sting-Rays is a popular pit stop for both travelers and locals, since the Cape Center also houses the Eastern Shore Pottery, a convenience store, the Exxon station, and an RV and boat storage facility. The restaurant serves breakfast, lunch, and dinner, with daily specials ranging from fried soft-shell crabs to hot turkey sandwiches. Think diner Eastern Shore–style!

Tail Waggers: Fido's Favorite Outings

Chatham Vineyards, 9232 Chatham Road, Machipongo (757-678-5588; www.chathamvineyards .com); June through August open daily 10–5; September through May Thursday to Monday 10–5, Sunday 12–5; free. A working farm for over 400 years, Chatham (pronounced CHAT-em) was named after William Pitt, the Earl of Chatham. The red-brick Federal-style house was built in 1818 and overlooks Church Creek. Two generations of the Wehner family have put their ex-pertise into the award-winning Chardonnay, Merlot, Cabernet Franc, Cabernet Sauvignon, and Petit Verdot vines. Complimentary tastings often include pairings of Chardonnay with two varieties (bay and sea) of locally harvested Shooting Point oysters, and you're sure to get a warm welcome from Wilbur, the winery's official canine greeter.

Visitors to Chatham Vineyards enjoy a wine tasting.

Eastern Shore of Virginia National Wildlife Refuge, 5003 Hallett Circle, Cape Charles (757-331-2760; www.fws.gov/northeast/easternshore/); Monday to Friday 8–4; free. If your pooch is a bird dog, he'll go crazy at one of the most important avian migration funnels on the continent. Depending on the time you visit, clouds of birds and butterflies hover over this refuge. Both the Butterfly Trail and the Wildlife Trail are easy hikes for you and Fido, making this a great place to take a break from the car and enjoy the natural beauty of the Eastern Shore.

Kiptopeke State Park, 3540 Kiptopeke Drive, Cape Charles (757-331-2267; www.dcr.virginia.gov/state_parks/kip.shtml); $2–4 parking and admission fees (additional fees for horses, fishing coupons); camping from $20 and cabins from $71 per night with additional pet fees of $5.25 and $10.50. With a beautiful beach, more than 4 miles of trails, and canine-friendly camping and cabins, Kiptopeke is also popular with birders and is the site of several bird-population studies. Whether you stop for a few hours or stay over, the park has excellent picnic facilities and fishing, as well as plenty of places for you and your four-legged explorer to roam.

Tangier Island, Tangier Ferry, Onancock (757-891-2505; www .tangierferry.com); $25 roundtrip. Once featured in a series of ESPN commercials, Tangier Island is only accessible by boat. Dogs are welcome on the ferry and the small, waterfront town is a great place to stroll and get a feel for the Eastern Shore's fishing heritage. Seemingly untouched by time, this is the place to see watermen going out in their small boats for crab and oysters the way Eastern Shore fishermen have done for centuries. Tangier Island residents are also known for their unique English Restoration–era dialect.

☺ Sweet Treats and Canine Chic: Where to Shop with Your BFF

gardenARTandGrocery, 44 King Street, Onancock (757-787-8818; www.gardenartandgrocery.com). The store's canine "clerk" Lulu, a Portugese water dog, will guide you through the garden décor if she's not napping in her favorite Adirondack chair. You can also pick up pet supplies and human food, along with local produce, fresh-baked bread, locally made soaps, and other gift items.

Howl Naturale, 4091 Main Street, Chincoteague Island (757-894-3126; www.howlnaturale.com). Chesapeake Bay Bridge-Tunnel staffers hand out over 1,000 pounds of Inge Veneziano's all-natural, seagull-shaped peanut

Jessie, one of Howl Naturale's best customers, loves to hang out by the statue of Misty in Chincoteague.

(Courtesy of Howl Naturale)

butter dog cookies each year. The handmade treats are made with 100 percent natural ingredients and no artificial colors, salt, or preservatives. Inspired by the equine heritage of the island, Veneziano also makes horse treats!

♛ A Day of Beauty: Best Pooch Primping

Eastern Shore Pet Spa, 34424 Lankford Hwy, Painter (757-442-7387; www.esanimalhospital.com). This full-service animal hospital also offers à la carte grooming services.

♥ Play Dates: Doggy Daycare

Eastern Shore Pet Spa, 34424 Lankford Hwy, Painter (757-442-7387; www.esanimalhospital.com). The region's largest animal clinic is also the local pet spa, with a full line of grooming services, as well as boarding facilities.

Paws Love Me, 299 Randolph Ave., Cape Charles (757-828-7297; www.pawsloveme.com). A member of Pet Sitters Associates and certified in pet first aid and pet CPR, Paws Love Me is a professional dog-walking and pet-sitting service that covers the Eastern Shore region.

Pick up a canine-inspired accent piece while shopping on the Eastern Shore.

Seaside Pet Resort, 29636 Seaside Rd., Melfa (757-787-8003; www .yourpetsresort.com); boarding from $17 per night; daycare from $15. Located on the southern end of the Eastern Shore about 45 minutes north of Cape Charles and 45 minutes south of Chincoteague, Seaside Pet Resort offers cage-free boarding in a state-of-the-art facility, as well as daycare and pet-sitting services. Boarders get their own rooms, supervised outdoor playtime, and personal leash walks if requested. A 24-hour attendant will even walk your pooch in the middle of the night if needed or cuddle up with homesick canines. Pet-sitting services at your residence are also available.

NOTE: Many of the B&Bs and inns listed in this chapter also offer on-site pet-sitting services.

Worth a Sitter: Sights to See without Fido

Chincoteague National Wildlife Refuge, 8231 Beach Road, Chincoteague Island (757-336-6122; www.fws.gov/northeast/chinco); $8 per vehicle; open daily. Pets are not even allowed in vehicles on the island (on the Virginia side), so leave your furry friend at daycare and spend an afternoon crabbing, fishing, swimming, biking, or hiking on this unspoiled island. Made famous by Marguerite Henry's classic book, *Misty of*

Crowds gather to watch the ponies swim ashore at the annual Chincoteague Pony Swim.

(Courtesy of the Chincoteague Chamber of Commerce)

Chincoteague, the wild ponies that roam the refuge are cared for by the Chincoteague Volunteer Fire Company. Legend has it that the ponies swam to shore in the 17th century from a Spanish galleon that sank nearby, but most historians believe the ponies are descendants of horses owned by early settlers of the Eastern Shore. On the last Wednesday and Thursday of July, the ponies are rounded up by "saltwater cowboys" for the Annual Pony Penning and Auction, where some are sold at auction to benefit the town's ambulance and fire services. Visit the 1867 Assateague Lighthouse or learn the history of Chincoteague and Assateague at the visitor center, where you can also sign up for a variety of guided tours.

Kayak Winery Tour (757-331-2680; www.southeastexpeditions.com); $85 per person. Spend a day paddling on the Chesapeake Bay, past serene inlets and islands and stop for a tour and tasting at Chatham Vineyards on Church Creek. Suitable for all skill levels, including beginners, the tour includes personal instruction, paddling gear, and a bottle of your favorite wine from the vineyard. Southeast Expeditions also offers kayak tours and rentals in Onancock and Chincoteague, as well as Cape Charles.

NASA Visitor Center at Wallops Flight Facility, Wallops Island (SR175); (757-824-2298; www.nasa.gov/centers/wallops/home/index.html); free; open 10 A.M.–4 P.M. Thursday to Monday. America's space program began at Wallops Island, a decade before NASA was born, and research rockets still depart from here on a regular basis, as well as rockets that resupply the International Space Station. With a permanent museum and many special exhibits, Wallops is poised to become an international tourism destination for fans of the space program. If you want to catch a sounding rocket launch, check the website for upcoming launch dates.

The Historic Triangle: Revolutionary R & R in Colonial Williamsburg, Jamestown, and Yorktown

America was born in the Historic Triangle of Jamestown, Williamsburg, and Yorktown. At Jamestown, 104 men and boys created the first permanent settlement in the New World. Colonial Williamsburg served as the political and cultural capital of the colony, and at Yorktown, the colonies gained their independence with the surrender of the British. All three are connected by a scenic 23-mile parkway that's a route to our past, and collectively the three towns are known as Colonial National Historical Park.

In 1607, three ships carrying the English settlers first landed at Cape Henry, but after a skirmish with the Natives, they reboarded the *Susan Constant*, *Godspeed*, and *Discovery* and headed upstream to find a more

(Continued on page 73)

Colonial Williamsburg's main street, Duke of Gloucester, is called DOG Street by the locals.

Fido 411

Here are some of the most important numbers to have when you arrive in the Historic Triangle:

✚ 24-hour Emergency Veterinarians

Anderson's Corner Animal Hospital, 8391 Richmond Road (757-566-2224; www.acah.com). While they're not a 24/7 emergency clinic, this full-service animal hospital has extended evening hours (7 A.M. to 8 P.M. Monday–Friday) and is open on Saturday (7 A.M. to 6 P.M.) and Sunday (8 A.M. to 6 P.M.). They're located at Anderson's Corner, at the intersection of routes 60 and 30.

Peninsula Emergency Veterinary Clinic, 1120 George Washington Memorial Highway (Rt 17 & Oyster Point Road), Yorktown (757-874-8115; www.peninsulaemergencyvet.com). Also referred to as the Animal Emergency Clinic, this is the closest 24-hour emergency veterinarian to the Historic Triangle area. Since they partner with 17 primary care veterinarians in the region, this is where you would be referred for an after-hours emergency.

Animal Poison Control Center—ASPCA (888-426-4435 or www.aspca.org/pet-care/poison-control/). If you think your pet may have ingested a poisonous substance or animal, help is available 24 hours a day, 365 days a year.

To find an emergency-care veterinarian from your smartphone, check the following websites for the closest location:

www.vetsnearyou.com, www.localvets.com, or **www.animalclinicsnear you.com** Enter the zip code of your location and it will bring up a list and map of the closest veterinarians.

🌙 24-hour Pharmacies

To find a 24-hour pharmacy, check the store-locator search on one of these websites:

CVS: www.cvs.com

Walgreens: www.walgreens.com

RX List: www.rxlist.com/pharmacy/local_locations_pharmacies.htm

D-Tails

Colonial Williamsburg Foundation www.history.org

Colonial Williamsburg Attractions/Booking www.colonialwilliamsburg.com

Colonial National Historical Park www.nps.gov/colo

Jamestown www.nps.gov/jame/

Official Jamestown Settlement and Yorktown Victory Center Visitor Center www.historyisfun.org

Preservation Virginia www.historicjamestowne.org

Yorktown www.visityorktown.org

Travel 411

Accommodations are centered in the Williamsburg area. Jamestown and Yorktown are nearby (6 miles and 10 miles, respectively), connected by the scenic Colonial Parkway, and easily reached for day trips, dining, or sightseeing excursions.

Bruton Parish Church has been holding services for over 300 years in Williamsburg and features an excellent gift shop with jewelry and crafts by local artists.

secure location on the banks of what became known as the James River. Archaeologists are still uncovering the remains of the original fort and its buildings on Historic Jamestowne Island. You and Fido are welcome to watch the ongoing digs and explore the riverfront site where it all began. If you visit in the late afternoon, you may see head archaeologist, William Kelso, strolling through the park with his canine companions. Adjacent to the island is the Jamestown Settlement, a living-history exhibit with costumed interpreters who re-create the life of the early settlers and the Native Americans who inhabited the region (unfortunately, your pooch can't accompany you to the Settlement).

A visit to Colonial Williamsburg, especially on a quiet day in the off-season, is as close as most of us will ever come to time travel. In the early morning, as you stroll down Duke of Gloucester Street with your best friend, the sounds of carriage wheels on cobblestones, the smell of wood smoke and musty boxwood, and the sight of workers in colonial costume hurrying to their posts will transport you to the 18th century. Once the largest and most populous city in the colony, and for a time the capital of Virginia, Williamsburg was restored by John D. Rockefeller Jr. In 1926, the pastor of Bruton Parish Church, Reverend A. R. Goodwin, approached Rockefeller about saving the historic buildings in the city. What began as a simple restoration project became the world's largest living-history museum, set on 301 acres and including hundreds of restored original structures, as well as recon-structed buildings to re-create Williamsburg as it was during the pivotal years

Local residents often walk their dogs along the Yorktown River.

of the colony and the Revolutionary War. Costumed interpreters at the trade shops demonstrate the techniques of the past, making everything from hats to jewelry, while daily street-theater performances draw visitors into the drama of the day, as carts drawn by oxen and horse-drawn carriages move through the town. Colonial "residents" roll hoops on the Palace Green or march regally in the Drum & Fife Corps.

Historic Yorktown, just 10 miles away on the Colonial Parkway, was the site of both an end and a beginning. When British General Cornwallis surrendered here, it marked the end of the Revolutionary War and the beginning of a nation. Picnic with your pooch on the banks of the York River near the cave where Cornwallis hid, or romp on the

A statue of Pocahontas commemorates the early colony.

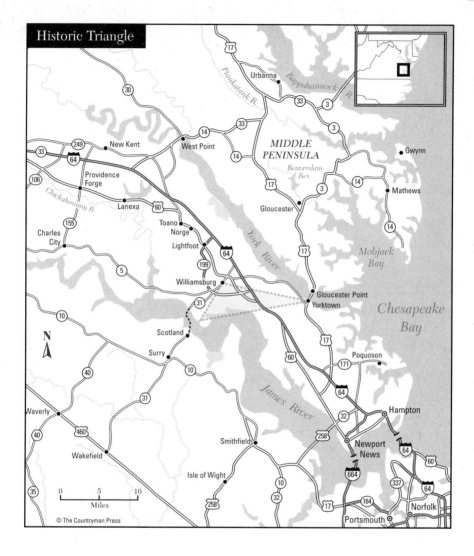

Historic Triangle

© The Countryman Press

private beach, enjoying views of the sailing schooners anchored at the dock.
Stroll through the historic area and stop for a sweet treat at the Cole Diggs
House, now home to a favorite local eatery, the Carrot Tree, or visit the
Victory Monument perched high above the river.

Collectively known as the Colonial National Historical Park, the three
major entities of the Historic Triangle—Jamestown, Yorktown, and Colonial
Williamsburg—are connected by the 23-mile Colonial Parkway. There is no
fee for driving or biking the parkway, but you can buy a Colonial Historical
Park Pass ($10, valid for seven days) that includes admission to Historic

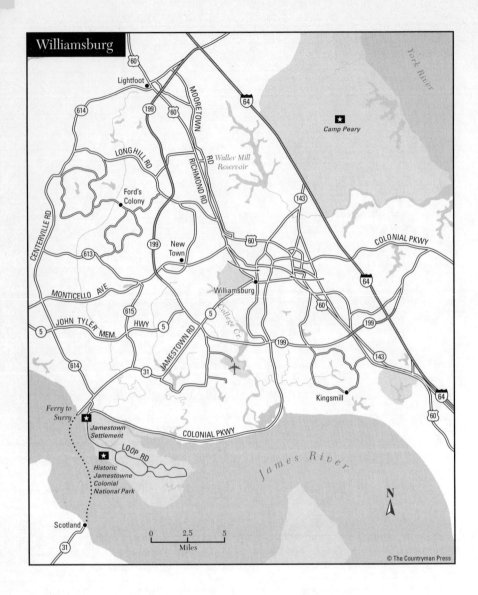

Jamestowne (the island) and the Yorktown Battlefield or you may use a
national park pass. There is an official visitor center at each of the three
gateways to the parkway. Most pet-friendly accommodations are located in
Williamsburg, but Jamestown and Yorktown are just a short drive away. If
you're exploring without your pal, you can take the free Historic Triangle
Shuttle. It runs from mid-March through early November, departing from
the Colonial Williamsburg Visitor Center every 30 minutes for Jamestown
and Yorktown.

Best Beds: Comfy Sleeps for You and Your Canine Family

Crowne Plaza, 6945 Pocahontas Trail (757-220-2250; www.crowne plaza.com); from $108 per night. This modern hotel is located on the Fort Magruder Battleground, within easy walking distance of the Colonial area. Pets up to 40 pounds are welcome with a nonrefundable $45 pet deposit and a limit of two pets per room. With an indoor and an outdoor pool, fitness center, lighted tennis courts, and business center, the Crowne Plaza's modern amenities blend harmoniously with an updated Colonial décor.

Holiday Inn Patriot, 3032 Richmond Road (757-565-2600; www.hipatriot.com); from $110 per night. Casual and comfortable, this hotel is a bit farther from CW (about a 15-minute drive) but has tons of amenities including complimentary computer access in the lobby area, indoor and outdoor pools, a restaurant and casual bar & grill, and a fitness center. If you like to shop, you'll be close to the megasized outlet malls and discount stores. There are no size restrictions, but you'll pay an extra $15 per night per pet.

Marriott Residence Inn, 1648 Richmond Road (757-941-2000; www.marriott.com); from $159 per night. Make yourself at home in one of the 108 suites at the Residence Inn, all with full kitchens and a bright and airy décor that's more like a vacation apartment than a hotel room. A $75 nonrefundable pet fee covers your entire stay, and there are no size or weight restrictions.

Williamsburg Inn, 300 East Francis Street (757-229-1000; www.colonialwilliamsburg.com); from $400 per night. Listed on the National Register of Historic Places and a member of the Leading Hotels of the World, the Williamsburg Inn was built in 1937 by John D. Rockefeller Jr. You and your pooch will be treated like a Rockefeller at this gracious, five-star resort that has hosted the rich, the royal, and the powerful from around the globe. Expect stunning Colonial décor and stellar service from this official Colonial Williamsburg hotel. Small pets are welcome with an additional $50-per-night fee and a refundable $500 damage deposit. Guests at the hotel get a special discount on passes to Colonial Williamsburg: $29 gets you a pass good for the length of your stay and admission to the 35 exhibition sites and 16 trade shops in CW, plus complimentary bus transportation and a 25 percent discount on special evening programs. You also get preferred dining reservations at CW taverns and complimentary delivery to the

The five-star Williamsburg Inn is always beautiful, but especially so during the holidays, when it hosts a special tree lighting.

inn of your purchases at official Colonial Williamsburg stores.

Williamsburg Manor, 600 Richmond Road (757-220-8011; www.williamsburg-manor.com); from $149 per night. Four-legged guests are welcome (with a reservation) with no additional fee or restrictions at this Colonial bed & breakfast located just past the College of William & Mary and within walking distance of Colonial Williamsburg. Book early and ask for the Palace Chambers Yellow room on the ground floor, overlooking the lush gardens. Don't be thrown off if the phone is answered "Williamsburg Occasions": the owners also run a local catering company.

Williamsburg Sampler, 922 Jamestown Road (757-255-0398; www.williamsburgsampler.com); from $145 per night. Also within walking distance of CW and owned by the same folks that operate Williamsburg Manor, the Sampler has six chamber rooms and suites, some with fireplaces or with access to the rooftop garden. The inn is furnished with period antiques, pewter, and four-poster beds, but their claim to fame is their signature SkipLunch Breakfast, an extravaganza of home-baked goods and hot entrées served by candlelight. If you can't eat it all, take a doggy bag back to your elegant room for your buddy. Pets are welcome with no additional fees or restrictions, but as with Williamsburg Manor, you must reserve a spot for your four-legged friend in advance.

Best Bowls: Restaurants Worth a Sitter

Berret's Seafood Restaurant and Taphouse Grill, 199 South Boundary Street, Williamsburg (757-253-1847; www.berrets.com). Located in Merchants Square, just a block from the Historic District, Berret's and the Taphouse Grill have been voted "best of" for a decade by local residents. Serving up fresh catch from the nearby Atlantic Ocean, Chesapeake Bay, and James and York Rivers, you'll find a seasonal menu with shad roe, softshell crabs, and trout in the spring, flounder and bluefish in the summer, and a Virginia specialty, rockfish, in the fall. The Taphouse Grill is an outdoor bar where you can kick back with a cold brew and some steamers or peel 'n eat shrimp and enjoy live entertainment on weekends.

Chowning's Tavern, 109 East Duke of Gloucester Street, Williamsburg (757-229-2141; www.colonial williamsburg.com). Another official tavern of CW, Chowning's (pronounced CHOO-nings by historians) was an "ordinary," or tavern for regular folks. Party like an 18th-century Williamsburg resident at

the evening gambols. Grab a pint of ale and a fistful of Virginia peanuts while you learn the games and songs of the era. The tavern serves a light menu that's a combination of historic and modern bar food: Brunswick stew and Welsh rarebit for those who want to immerse themselves in time travel, and wings and barbeque for more modern palates.

Christiana Campbell's Tavern, 101 South Waller Street, Williamsburg (757-229-2141; www.colonial williamsburg.com). In 1771, widow Christiana Campbell opened a tavern to support her two young daughters. George Washington and other notable gentlemen from the colony often spent an evening dining or drinking and gambling in the public room. Williamsburg was the capital of Virginia, so business was booming at Campbell's, but when the government moved to Richmond, Mrs. Campbell retired from the hospitality business. The tavern was reconstructed from artifacts found both on the site and in other areas of Williamsburg, and today specializes in the type of seafood Washington and his cronies may have dined on in the 18th century. Try the fried oyster Randolph appetizer, and for an entrée the "fricassy" of shrimp, scallops and lobster, or the crabcakes with ham lardons and spicy mustard.

If your kids misbehave, you can put them in the stocks next to the Courthouse.

Fat Canary, 410 West Duke of Gloucester Street, Williamsburg (757-229-3333; www.fatcanary williamsburg.com). The Fat Canary has been awarded the AAA Four Diamond designation for the past seven consecutive years, and a glance at the menu easily explains the kudos. This is a foodie favorite, serving an impressive list of wines from Europe and Napa (sadly no Virginia vintages) and a seasonal menu that changes daily with esoteric entrées from fricassee of rabbit, roasted quail, and guinea fowl to seared foie gras and inventively prepared seafood.

Old Chickahominy House, 1211 Jamestown Road, Williamsburg (757-229-4689; www.oldchicka

hominy.com). Just a mile or so from the historic area, Old Chickahominy House is known for its ham biscuits and homemade pie. Enjoy a hearty breakfast in the homey dining room, and then shop the eclectic three-level antiques and gift shop in the rest of the old house. For many years, travelers made a point of stopping in to say hello to the resident feline, Mr. Biscuit, who had an annual birthday bash attended by locals and visitors alike. Today, Miss Melinda is the chatty cat you'll usually find holding court in the gift shop.

Riverwalk Restaurant, 323 Water Street, Yorktown (757-875-1522; http://riverwalkrestaurant.net). Enjoy great seafood (the restaurant

Lunch to Go

The Historic Triangle is filled with scenic outdoor spots just begging for a picnic, so try one of these insider favorites for an alfresco lunch.

Carrot Tree, 1782 Jamestown Road, Williamsburg (757-229-0957) Dale House Café in Historic Jamestown (757-229-1170), Cole Diggs House, 411 Main Street, Yorktown (757-988-1999; www.carrottreekitchens.com /williamsburg). With three locations in the Historic Triangle and a sinful array of homemade treats (carrot cake is the specialty!), the Carrot Tree offers boxed lunches for under $10 that include a sandwich, side, and brownie. The Yorktown location in the historic Cole Diggs house even has picnic tables in the yard where you and your pooch can dine.

The Cheese Shop, 410 West Duke of Gloucester Street, Williamsburg (757-220-0298; www.cheeseshopwilliamsburg.com). You'll probably have to wait in line for one of the Cheese Shop's scrumptious deli sandwiches, since this is one of the most popular spots in town, but if you call in your order in advance, you can pick it up at the side window. With a wide array of cheeses, wine and beer, charcuterie, and salads to choose from, you can create an alfresco lunch or dinner to suit your mood. Toss a blanket on the Palace Green for an impromptu picnic lunch or savor the serenity of the sunken garden behind the Christopher Wren Building on the campus of William & Mary.

The Carrot Tree in the Cole Diggs House in Yorktown has picnic tables where you and your pooch can share lunch.

is owned by the same folks that run Berret's in Williamsburg) while you dine overlooking the York River at Riverwalk Restaurant. Locals rave about the crabcakes and the huge Hot Brown turkey sandwich that's big enough to share.

The Trellis, 403 West Duke of Gloucester Street, Williamsburg (757-229-8610; www.thetrellis .com). One of the first fine-dining outlets in Williamsburg, the Trellis has been a local favorite for three decades, but don't expect stuffy cuisine; the focus is on locally sourced ingredients and artisan farmers. You'll find creative starters like the Farmer's Plate with slow-roasted rabbit terrine and fresh headcheese, and an oyster BLT, fresh fried oysters with bacon, tomatoes, and microgreens. Entrées like fresh trout with crab and crayfish stuffing or Atlantic cedar-planked salmon showcase the region's bounty. Winner of the Wine Spectator Award of Excellence, the restaurant also offers a tasting menu with wine pairings.

Tail Waggers: Fido's Favorite Outings

Colonial Williamsburg Walk

(www.colonialwilliamsburg.com); free. Covering 301 acres, the Historic Area of Colonial Williamsburg features 88 original 18th-century structures, and hundreds of re-created buildings including homes, trade shops, the Governor's Palace, and the Capitol Building. You'll see lots of four-legged tourists as you explore, especially on Duke of Gloucester Street (DOG Street, as the locals call it). It's less crowded on the side streets and in the residential area near the Magazine or the Williamsburg Inn. Watch out for horse-drawn carriages and the occasional team of oxen led by costumed interpreters (and also watch where you step). Every day in front of the Courthouse, a live street-theater performance called Revolutionary City tells the stories of Colonial times. Since the actors often call on participation from the audience, you and Fido need to be prepared to play your part. During

Duke of Gloucester (aka DOG) Street, is lined with shops and restuarants.

Fido and his friend check out the ongoing archaelogical dig at Historic Jamestowne.

the Christmas holiday season, the colonial homes and shops are decorated with all-natural wreaths and arrangements made from fruits, seeds, and greenery.

Historic Jamestowne, 1368 Colonial Parkway, Jamestown Island (757-229-9776; www.historic-jamestowne.org); national park pass or from $10. 8:30 A.M. to 4:30 P.M. daily. Located on the western end of the Colonial Parkway, Historic Jamestowne (also called "the Island" by locals) is the original site of the first permanent English settlement and is operated jointly by the National Park Service and Preservation Virginia. On the Island, you and your four-legged friend can walk in your ancestor's footsteps and paw prints, and explore the ongoing digs on the banks of the James River. Remains of the original fort and earliest church have been uncovered, and treasured artifacts from the early colonists' lives are discovered daily. If you're there in the late afternoon, you may see head archaeologist, William Kelso, walking his two best friends around the grounds.

Williamsburg Farmers Market, 402 West Duke of Gloucester Street (in Merchants Square between Henry and Boundary Streets); (757-259-3768; www.williamsburgfarmersmarket.com); free; Saturdays 8 A.M. to noon April to October; special holiday markets in November and December. You and your furry friend can sample some of Virginia's finest produce, baked goods, jams, and other culinary treats at the weekly farmers market in Merchants Square. During the holidays, gorgeous handcrafted wreaths and holiday arrangements are hard to resist. Parking is free in the Francis Street lot until noon.

William & Mary, Duke of Gloucester Street (www.wm.edu). Fido will enjoy this educational stroll through the campus of the second-oldest college in the United States. Start at the Sir Christopher Wren Building, the oldest college building in America and the oldest of Williamsburg's restored buildings. In 1693, King William III and Queen Mary II signed the charter for the college, but due to an Indian uprising, construction on the first building was delayed. Designed by notable English architect Christopher Wren, the building, known originally simply as the College Building, was started in 1695 before Williamsburg was even a town. Follow the brick path to the back of the building and the Sunken Garden to the Old Campus and the six buildings surrounding the garden. William & Mary is nicknamed "the Alma Mater of a Nation" due to its close ties to our founding fathers. George Washington received his surveyor's license from the school, and presidents Thomas Jefferson, John Tyler,

DOG Street

The main street in Colonial Williamsburg, Duke of Gloucester, is often referred to by locals as DOG Street, and judging by the number of canines you'll see strolling on a pretty day, it's a fitting moniker. Running from the Christopher Wren Building to the Capitol, Dog Street is lined with colonial homes, trade shops, taverns, and gardens. Take a turn around the Palace Green or explore the Sunken Garden behind the Wren Building.

and James Monroe all received their undergraduate degrees from W & M. It's also the home of the first law school in America and the first Greek letter society, Phi Beta Kappa, founded in 1776. Circle around the University Center to the Crim Dell Bridge, voted the second-most-romantic spot on a college campus. Continue past the Alumni House and Zable Stadium to return to the Richmond Road side of the Wren Building.

Yorktown Riverwalk Landing, 425 Water Street, Yorktown (757-890-3500; www.riverwalklanding.com); free parking. After you explore the historic buildings and victory statue in the old town, walk down

Alice helps her human, Jill, at Patriot Tours and Provisions in Yorktown's Riverwalk Landing.

the hill to picnic by the water near the Cornwallis Cave. The Riverwalk dining, shopping, and entertainment complex is located on the banks of the York River, with scenic views of replica sailing schooners and the Middle Peninsula. Stroll along Water Street and pick up a doggy Frisbee for your pal at Patriot Tours and Provisions, where you can say hello to the store owners' canine clerk, or grab an ice cream at Ben & Jerry's.

☺ Sweet Treats and Canine Chic: Where to Shop with your BFF

Nautical Dog, 5104 North Main Street (757-220-2001; www .nauticaldogwilliamsburg.com). Take your four-legged friend on a shopping spree at this bow-wow boutique and bakery in New Town's shopping and entertainment district. Pick up fresh doggy treats, canine couture and accessories, or creative gifts for dog lovers like wine bags decorated with your favorite breeds.

◉ Big-Box Stores

Petco www.petco.com, 6610 Mooretown Road (757-564-3560).

PetSmart www.petsmart.com, 4900 Monticello Avenue (757-259-1630).

🐾 A Day of Beauty: Best Pooch Primping

Paws for Reflection, 5242 Olde Towne Road (757-253-1018; www .pfr-williamsburg.com). Offering low-stress grooming with set appointment times so your dog won't

The Nautical Dog is a favorite shopping spot for Williamsburg dogs.

You and your pal can get a taste of life in the 18th century with a stroll through Colonial Williamsburg.

sit in a cage all day, PFR assigns one groomer to your pooch, who handles everything from bath, brush, and nail trim to hand drying. The shop also sells high-quality organic and raw dog foods.

NOTE: Grooming services are also available at PetSmart, Petco, and many of the local veterinary clinics.

♥ Play Dates: Doggy Daycare

The Pet Resort at Greensprings, 2878 Monticello Avenue (757-220-2880; www.williamsburgpetresort .com); boarding from $25 per night; daycare from $20 per day. Situated on 15 acres close to Colonial Williamsburg, the Pet Resort offers both boarding and daycare, with both indoor and outdoor play areas and personal service like one-on-one walks if requested. Boarding accommodations range from economy rooms to luxury suites, with special ARP (Association of Retired Pets) rooms for senior guests.

Smiley Pets (757-817-3821; http://smileypetsitting.webs.com); from $15. Smiley Pets offers dog-walking and pet-sitting services in the Historic Triangle area. They'll even take your pooch on field trips to the park or the beach.

Worth a Sitter: Sights to See without Fido

Candlelight Concerts at Bruton Parish Church, 331 West Duke of Gloucester Street (757-229-2891; www.brutonparish.org); free (donation recommended); 8 P.M. Saturdays with additional concerts Tuesday and Thursday March to December. This historic Episcopal Church has been an active parish for more than 300 years and their candlelight concert series of 18th-century organ music is stunning, especially during the holiday season.

Colonial Williamsburg Visitor Pass (1-800-447-8679; www .colonialwilliamsburg.com); from $39.95; open daily. While you can stroll all through the Historic Area with Fido, you should also see the interiors of the Colonial buildings like the Palace and the Capitol, visit the trade shops to watch craftsmen create everything from silver jewelry to hats the way it was done in the 18th century, or take a leisurely carriage ride around the town. Start at the Colonial Williamsburg Visitor Center with the classic movie *Williamsburg: The Story of a Patriot,* starring a young Jack Lord (*Hawaii Five-O* fame). There are many discounts available for seniors, military personnel, first responders (fire, EMT, law enforcement), educators, and students, and if you stay at an official CW hotel like the Williamsburg Inn, you can get a length of stay pass for just $29.95, plus discounts on evening programs like the ghost tour. Buy passes online, at the visitor center, or from your concierge if you stay at an official CW hotel.

Jamestown Settlement and Yorktown Victory Center (757-253-4838 or toll-free (888-593-4682; www.historyisfun.org); from $20 combo pass; open 9 A.M. to 5 P.M. daily (until 6 P.M. June 15 through August 15); closed Christmas and New Year's. While you can use a national park pass to enter Historic Jamestowne Island, operated by the National Park Service and Preservation Virginia, you'll need an admission ticket to visit either the Jamestown Settlement with its re-created fort, Powhatan Indian village and recon-

structed sailing ships (*Susan Constant, Godspeed,* and *Discovery*) or to tour the Yorktown Victory Center. In addition to the comprehensive museum, which chronicles America's fight for independence, Yorktown also has outdoor living-history experiences, including a re-created Continental Army encampment and an 18th-century farm. There are a variety of combination passes (including one that includes Colonial Williamsburg) and discounts available.

Yorktown Schooner *Alliance*, 425 Water Street, Yorktown (757-639-1233; www.sailyorktown.com); from $30 per person, April to early November. Sail into history on the schooners *Alliance* or *Serenity* with a two-hour cruise on the York River. Help trim the sails, glide by historic battle sites, or relax and enjoy local wildlife from dolphins to osprey. Cruises depart from the Riverwalk Landing Pier.

On the island, a cannon points toward the battlefied.

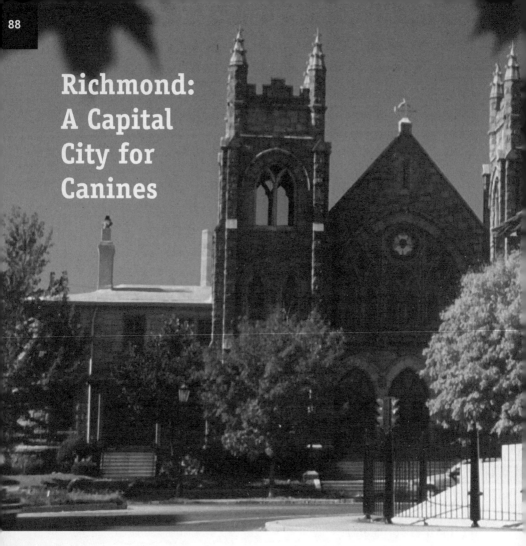

Richmond: A Capital City for Canines

Although William Byrd II named the city Richmond because it reminded him of Richmond, England, on the Thames River, the resemblance ends there. The state capital of Virginia and former capital of the Confederacy is a study in contrasts, with an urban core studded with more than 80 historic attractions, many of them related to the Civil War (or as we Virginians call it, the War Between the States), as well as an abundance of recreational parks and outdoor adventures. And while the James River in 1737 may have re-minded Byrd of the Thames, it's doubtful that Richmond, England, has Class IV whitewater rapids in the midst of its downtown district or a somewhat painful history as one of the main points of entry for the slave trade from Africa.

(Continued on page 91)

The only street in America listed on the National Register of Historic Places, Richmond's Monument Avenue is a tribute to Confederate heroes.

(Courtesy of Richmond Metropolitan Convention & Visitors Bureaus)

Fido 411

Here are some of the most important numbers to have when you arrive in Richmond:

✚ 24-hour Emergency Veterinarians

Deer Run Animal Medical Center, 13821 Fribble Way, Midlothian (804-639-3900; www.deerrunanimalmedical.com). Located in Midlothian on the south side of Richmond, Deer Run offers emergency care 24/7. Local veterinarians refer clients to Deer Run for round-the-clock emergency care, and also recommend them for special-needs pet boarding.

Dogwood Veterinary Emergency & Specialty Center, 5918 West Broad Street, Richmond (804-716-4700; www.dvesc.com). Located just west of the Museum District on Broad Street, Dogwood has specialists on call for all types of emergencies 24/7.

Veterinary Emergency & Specialty Centers (VESC), 3312 West Cary Street, Carytown (804-353-9000; http://animal-emergency.com/) and on the Southside, 2460 Colony Crossing Place, Midlothian (804-744-9800). Both locations of VESC, one on the west end of town and one on the south side of the city, offer 24-hour emergency services daily.

Veterinary Referral & Critical Care (VRCC), 1596 Hockett Road, Manakin-Sabot (804-784-8722; www.vrccvet.com). VRCC is on the far west side of Richmond in Manakin-Sabot, offering emergency and critical care 24/7.

Animal Poison Control Center—ASPCA, (888-426-4435 or www.aspca .org/pet-care/poison-control/). If you think your pet may have ingested a poisonous substance or animal, help is available 24 hours a day, 365 days a year.

To find an emergency care veterinarian from your smartphone, check the following websites for the closest location:

www.vetsnearyou.com, **www.localvets.com**, or **www.animalclinic snearyou.com** Enter the zip code of your location and it will bring up a list and map of the closest veterinarians.

24-hour Pharmacies

To find a 24-hour pharmacy, check the store-locator search on one of these websites:

CVS: www.cvs.com

Walgreens: www.walgreens.com

RX List: www.rxlist.com/pharmacy/local_locations_pharmacies.htm

D-Tails

Civil War Traveler Richmond www.civilwartraveler.com/EAST/VA/va-central/richmond.html

Virginia Civil War Sesquicentennial www.virginiacivilwar.org/committee events.php

Richmond Metropolitan Convention & Visitors Bureau www.visit richmondva.com

Richmond Pet Lovers www.richmondpetlovers.com

History Hounds http://richmondhistorycenter.com/calendar/history-hounds-oct

Travel 411

Virginia Commonwealth University is spread throughout downtown Richmond, so during the school year (September–May), traffic can be congested in this area. Be prepared to pay for parking (meters and garages) in the downtown area (your hotel may charge for parking as well). And, as in any large urban center, be careful while walking around the city, especially after dark.

But Richmond is also a city of firsts: fielding the first African American governor in the country, Douglas Wilder, and the first African American tennis player to win the US Open, Arthur Ashe. The city also had both the first hospital and the first television station in the South. Going even further back, George Washington designed America's first canal system, the Kanawha, and Thomas Jefferson designed the State Capitol. At Virginia's oldest wooden church, St. John's, in one of Richmond's oldest neighborhoods, Church Hill, a young Patrick Henry gave his rousing speech, "Give me liberty or give me death," convincing his peers that the American Revolution was the answer to England's tyranny.

Church Hill is lined with 18th- and 19th-century homes.

(Courtesy of Richmond Metropolitan Convention & Visitors Bureau)

After decades of urban decay, Richmond has reinvented itself with a renaissance of art and architecture, as well as a renewed commitment to its history. The Manchester Slave Trail and Slavery Reconciliation Statue tell the story of the abomination of the slave trade in the city, while museums like the Maggie L. Walker National Historic Site celebrate African American leaders and entrepreneurs. Arthur Ashe has a statue on Monument Avenue, the only street in America designated as a Historic Landmark, as does Robert E. Lee, for both are celebrated equally for their contributions in eras that are diametrically opposed. The campus of Virginia Commonwealth University, known throughout the world for its art programs, is spread across downtown, and the Virginia Museum of Fine Arts, after a multimillion-dollar renovation and expansion, is truly one of the country's most magnificent art destinations. In fact, one might say that it's these centuries-old contrasts that have given birth to the current city that is mindful of both its past and its future.

Virginia has more Civil War battlefields than any other state, and as the capital of the Confederacy, Richmond is at the epicenter of the multiyear Civil War Sesquicentennial. Special events and programs, battle reenactments, and museum exhibits will run through 2015, with a focus on interpreting the

The History Hounds program at the Richmond Valentine History Center takes both four- and two-legged visitors on narrated strolls through Richmond's historic districts.

(Courtesy of Richmond Valentine History Center)

10 Free Pet-Friendly Historic Sites

Belle Isle and Brown's Island
www.trails.com/tcatalog_trail.aspx?trailid=HGD164-005

Canal Walk www.richmondriverfront.com/canalwalk.shtml

Chimborazo Medical Museum www.nps.gov/rich

Cold Harbor Battlefield www.nps.gov/rich

Fort Harrison www.nps.gov/rich

Glendale/Malvern Hill Battlefields www.nps.gov/rich

Richmond National Battlefield Park Visitor Center www.nps.gov/rich

Confederate War Memorial Chapel www.richmondgov.com/visitor/monumentsmemorials.aspx

Hollywood Cemetery www.richmondgov.com/visitor/monuments memorials.aspx

Virginia War Memorial www.richmondgov.com/visitor/monuments memorials.aspx

NOTE: Well-behaved, leashed pets are welcome on the grounds of these sites, but only service dogs are allowed in museum exhibit areas. The park service does ask owners to keep dogs off battlefield earthworks.

experiences and effects of this divisive struggle on the North, the South, and the African Americans who were finally freed. The fall of Richmond was the precursor to Lee's surrender at Appomattox, and standing at Richmond National Battlefield, looking at the trestles crossing the James River, one can almost hear the rumbling of the train carrying Confederate President Jefferson Davis out of the devastated city.

Fido's Richmond is as diverse as the city itself, with a cornucopia of canine activities. Richmond History Tours, a service of the Valentine Richmond History Center, include several "History Hounds" tours throughout the year, where locals and visitors can bring their four-legged friends to explore historic neighborhoods and attractions. Take your pal to Belle Island for a picnic, stroll along the canals designed by George Washington on the Canal Walk, or head to "Yappy Hour" at nearby James River Cellars Winery. You'll find a wide range of pet-friendly accommodations, from the historic and elegant Jefferson Hotel, one of only 33 hotels in the United States to hold both the five-star and five-diamond designations, to the Euro-chic Aloft Hotel in Richmond's West End, a dining and shopping mecca.

Nearby and Noteworthy

CONFEDERATE MUST-SEE SIGHTS IN PETERSBURG: PAMPLIN PARK,
PETERSBURG BATTLEFIELD, AND BLANDFORD CHURCH

Civil War explorers will definitely want to add a day trip to Petersburg to
their itinerary. An easy drive from Richmond, **Petersburg National
Battlefield** (www.nps.gov/pete) was the site of the longest battle of the
Civil War, a siege that lasted nine months and claimed 70,000 casualties.
When Ulysses Grant finally cut off Petersburg's supply lines, Richmond fell,
and six days later, Lee surrendered. **Pamplin Historical Park** (www.pamplin
park.org) is the home of the National Museum of the Civil War Soldier,
Tudor Hall Plantation, an exhibit of military fortifications, and several in-
terpretive trails through the Breakthrough Battlefield. **Historic Blandford
Church and Cemetery** (www.petersburg-va.org/tourism/bcemetery.asp)
is a bit off the beaten path, but worth a visit to see the stunning collection of 15 stained-glass windows designed by Louis Tiffany. Legend has
it that the women of the church, who raised the money for the windows,
also started the custom of Memorial Day in 1866 to honor the 30,000
Confederate soldiers buried on Memorial Hill.

Getting to Richmond

The Richmond region, a transition point between Virginia's Tidewater region
and the rolling hills of the Piedmont, is within a day's drive of half of the US
population and an easy drive from several of Virginia's most popular vacation
spots: 50 miles from the Historic Triangle, 100 miles south of Washington,
DC, and just a few hours west of the Atlantic coast. The city sits at the intersection of Interstates 95 (north-south) and 64 (east-west). I-295 is a beltway
loop around the city, while SR 288 runs from I-95 in Chesterfield County to
US 250 (also known as Broad Street in town) in Goochland. Toll roads include
the Downtown Expressway and Powhite Parkway, with fees ranging from 20
cents to $2.70 (EZPass is accepted).

Travel to the plantations of Berkeley and Shirley on scenic SR 5, which
runs from Church Hill all the way to Williamsburg, or try US 60 (east-west)
to take a break from interstate driving. US 1 is also an alternative for north-
south travel and easy to access from I-95 if you come across a traffic jam or
accident, since it runs parallel to the interstate. The charming railroad town
of Ashland, where Patrick Henry honed his craft at the historic Hanover

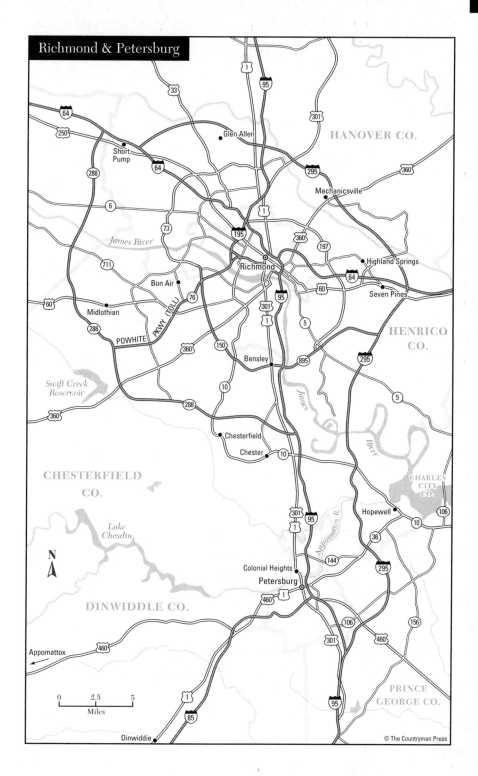

Richmond & Petersburg

HANOVER CO.

Glen Allen

Short Pump

Mechanicsville

James River

Richmond

Highland Springs

Bon Air

Seven Pines

HENRICO CO.

Midlothian

POWHITE PKWY (TOLL)

Bensley

Swift Creek Reservoir

James River

Chesterfield

Chester

CHESTERFIELD CO.

CHARLES CITY CO.

Lake Chesdin

Hopewell

Appomattox R.

N

Colonial Heights

Petersburg

DINWIDDLE CO.

Appomattox

0   2.5   5
Miles

PRINCE GEORGE CO.

Dinwiddie

© The Countryman Press

Tater lives in Church Hill, the oldest neighborhood in Richmond, and loves to go the park by the Chimborazo Medical Museum. (Courtesy of Tamra Talmadge-Anderson)

Courthouse, is just 20 miles north of Richmond, and Petersburg, besieged by the Union Army in 1864, is about 30 minutes south on I-95. If you fly in to Richmond International Airport (RIC), you'll see signs on your way to the baggage claim on the lower level for the "Pet Relief Area," a small fenced enclosure beside the parking garage.

Getting Around Town: Richmond Neighborhoods

If you hear a local say they live on the "Southside," they mean south of the James River, which bisects the city. Most of Richmond's historic attractions are north of the river, in and around the downtown district. The Court End district, an eight-block area north of Broad Street and the Capitol, contains several National Historic Landmarks including the Confederate White House and three museums (including the Valentine History Center). Parking is extremely difficult in this area, due in large part to Richmond's VCU Medical Center, which has grown up around the site of the Museum of the Confederacy and the Confederate White House. About a mile east of the Court End district is one of the oldest neighborhoods in the city, Church Hill. With excellent views of the city from the hilltop, Church Hill is home to historic St. John's Church, where Patrick Henry made history with his "Give me liberty . . ." speech, the Chimborazo Medical Museum, and streets lined with 19th-century homes.

Richmond is built on a grid system, but the tricky part is navigating the many one-way streets. Running east-west, Main Street is one-way heading west beginning at 14th Street. Main runs through the residential neighborhood known as the Fan, full of lovely Victorian-era homes and trendy eateries, while Broad Street west takes you through the downtown corridor and into the Museum District. A block north of the Fan, Monument Avenue, with its stately homes and statues, runs both east and west. Franklin Street runs east through the heart of the Virginia Commonwealth University campus and past the historic Jefferson Hotel. Cary Street also runs east-west, but is one-way heading east. On the far west end of Cary Street is the popular dining and shopping district known as Carytown, and between 12th and 15th Streets, the cobblestone blocks mark the shopping and dining district known as Shockoe Slip, once the city's commercial slave-trading district. Below the Slip is Shockoe Bottom, where the 17th Street Farmers Market has been operating since 1775. There are several excellent restaurants in this area as well.

Best Beds: Comfy Sleeps For You and Your Canine Family

Aloft Richmond West, 3939 Duckling Drive, Glen Allen (804-433-1888; www.alofthotels.com/Richmond); from $119 per night. Located in the trendy West End of Richmond about 20 minutes from downtown, known for its shopping and dining, Aloft is the American equivalent of Euro-chic design hotels. Modern to the max, Aloft also loves pets and has a special "Arf Program" that provides beds, bowls, and treats for four-legged guests up to 40 pounds with no additional fees. As part of the Starwood Group, Aloft accepts points for upgrades and free stays.

The Berkeley Hotel, 1200 East Cary Street (888-780-4422; www.berkeleyhotel.com); from $159 per night. This AAA four-diamond boutique hotel is located in the heart of downtown Richmond within walking distance of shops, restaurants, and many attractions. Pets 25 pounds and under are welcome with a onetime, nonrefundable fee of $50, and scenic Canal Walk is just a few blocks away for those leisurely morning strolls. Traditionally decorated rooms are comfortable but on the smaller side, this being an urban property, so you may want to opt for a suite.

DoubleTree by Hilton, 301 West Franklin Street (804-644-9871; www.doubletree.hilton.com); from $107 per night. With a convenient downtown location, complimentary high-speed Internet, and a complimentary shuttle within a 3-mile radius of the property, the Double-Tree welcomes pets up to 60 pounds with a onetime, nonrefundable fee of $50 per stay. If you're bringing a car, check out the "Park and Stay" package, which includes valet parking for your vehicle.

The Jefferson Hotel, 101 West Franklin Street (804-649-4750; www.jeffersonhotel.com); from $210 per night. One of the best hotels in America, with both a five-star and five-diamond rating (we can add five-woof to those!), the Jefferson is also a historic attraction in Richmond. Built in 1895 by Lewis Ginter, this beaux-arts gem has hosted presidents and royalty for over a century, including "the King," Elvis Presley. The life-sized Edward Valentine statue of Thomas Jefferson commands the Palm Court Lobby, which is ringed with Louis Tiffany windows, and is the location of a formal afternoon tea on weekends. The grand staircase leading to the lower lobby inspired an urban legend that *Gone with the Wind* moviemakers used it as their inspiration for the famous Rhett-Scarlett scene, and a mini-museum tells these and other stories of the

The Jefferson Hotel's grand staircase looks like it's right out of *Gone With the Wind*.

(Courtesy of The Jefferson Hotel)

historic hotel. With true Southern hospitality, both you and your four-legged friends are warmly welcomed (no weight limits and a $50-per-night fee), and the concierge will be happy to arrange dog-walking and pet-sitting services while you're exploring Richmond. The hotel's complimentary limousine is available to take you where you need to go within a 5-mile radius of the property. The hotel has an indoor pool, fitness center, full-service salon, gift shop, florist, and two excellent restaurants that both pay homage to its namesake: TJ's on the lower lobby level serves the best hamburger in town, along with Virginia favorites like crabcakes, while Lemaire offers up farm-to-table New American cuisine from award-winning chef Walter Bundy. Check out the special packages that combine breakfast or dinner, hotel gift cards, and special amenities, often a better value than purchasing à la carte.

The Omni Hotel, 100 12th Street (804-344-7000; www.omnihotels .com); from $212 per night. Located in the heart of the down-

The Fur Ball: A Premier Canine Cotillion at the Jefferson Hotel

Every fall, Richmond Fidos and their friends fly into a frenzy of fashion panic for the season's biggest event. For more than a decade, the Richmond SPCA's Fur Ball has been the signature black-tie event for pets and their people, held at the elegant Jefferson Hotel. Guests make a grand entrance down the hotel's imposing staircase and enjoy a cocktail reception, seated dinner, and live auction. The benefit gala is the primary fundraiser for the SPCA's Cinderella Fund, which pays for the care and rehabilitation of sick, injured, and neonatal homeless animals at the shelter.

Every fall, the Richmond SPCA hosts the annual Fur Ball at the five-star Jefferson Hotel.
(Courtesy of the Richmond SPCA and The Jefferson Hotel)

The Jefferson Hotel is one of only 33 hotels in the country holding both the five-star and five-diamond designations, and is listed on the National Register of Historic Places. Opened in 1895, the Jefferson was the realization of a dream by Richmond's wealthiest resident, Lewis Ginter. A Renaissance man himself, Ginter hired the renowned architectural firm Carrere and Hastings (who also designed the beaux-arts New York Public Library building on Fifth Avenue) to create an elegant homage to Virginia's great statesman.

The Jefferson has always warmly welcomed pets and their people. In the early 20th century, the marble pools in the Palm Court were filled with alligators. According to the legend, travelers picked them up in Florida, but soon tired of them and left them in the fountains, while local residents enthusiastically also donated their reptilian pets. The gators frequently left the pools and went exploring, and one hotel anecdote describes an alligator who wandered into the library, where an elderly hotel guest mistook it for a footstool. The last alligator, Old Pompey, remained at the hotel until his death in 1948, and is honored with a statue in front of the hotel entrance.

www.richmondspca.org
www.jeffersonhotel.com

town district within walking distance of shops, restaurants, and attractions including the Capitol, the Omni's opulent marble lobby spills into the James Center so you don't have to leave the building to hit the Starbuck's or shop at the eclectic boutiques that circle the atrium. If Fido needs an outdoor break, there's a small park on the west side of the Center that you can access from the Atrium exit door, and Canal Walk is just a few blocks away for a longer stroll. The 361 guest rooms and suites are tasteful and traditional, many with views of the James River. Pets 25 pounds and under are welcome with a one-time, nonrefundable fee of $25, and the hotel provides a mat, bowls, and gift for Fido at check-in, as well as a Director of Pet Relations to assist with any pet services or questions. If you think you're hearing bells while staying here, don't worry: the James Center Carillon is right next door!

Westin Richmond, 6631 West Broad Street (804-282-8444; www .starwoodhotels.com); from $209 per night. Located off I-64 at the Glenside exit on the west side of Richmond, the contemporary Westin welcomes pets up to 40 pounds with no additional fees. When you make your reservation, don't forget to ask for Westin's trademark Heavenly pet bed for your pal!

Best Bowls: Restaurants Worth a Sitter

Acacia, 2601 West Cary Street (804-562-0138; www.acaciarestaurant .com). Located at the corner of Cary and Robinson in the charming Fan District, Acacia is a longtime local favorite, and Chef Dale Reitzer is one of Richmond's culinary superstars. Focusing on seafood and regional cuisine with a modern aesthetic, the menu here changes daily. The prix fixe menu, offered Monday through Thursday evenings and as an early-bird special on Friday and Saturday, is a great deal with your choice of starter (lobster vichyssoise anyone?), entrée (sautéed flounder, fried softshell crabs, pan-roasted bistro steak) and dessert (make mine dark chocolate cremeux!).

Chez Foushee, 203 North Foushee (804-648-3225; www.chezfoushee .com). This continentally inspired bistro is an arts district favorite, located in the heart of downtown and just blocks from the Broad Street galleries. Chez Foushee serves lunch on weekdays, brunch on Sundays, and dinner on Friday and Saturday nights, and also offers carryout if you want stylish picnic fare for an alfresco lunch. Try the house paté de campagne with cornichons for upscale take-out, or dine in on seared sea scallops with foie gras in a Riesling reduction or crispy duck leg confit with sherried fig compote.

Julep's, 1719 East Franklin Street (804-377-3968; http://juleps .net/). The New Southern cuisine of Julep's, located in a renovated historic commercial building in Shockoe Bottom, is served in an elegant dining room, where the food is the star and the wine list regularly wins kudos from *Wine Spectator*. Julep's amps up the volume on Southern favorites from fried green tomatoes and shrimp & grits to low country bouillabaisse and pork chops.

Lemaire, 101 West Franklin Street (804-649-4629; http:// lemairerestaurant.com). Chef Walter Bundy has been a leader in the Richmond culinary community for the farm-to-table movement, and even has his own urban garden that supplies the restaurant with fresh herbs and vegetables. Lemaire is located in the historic Jefferson Hotel, and Bundy's menu is worthy of TJ himself, with New American twists on regional fare from Eastern Shore oysters to maple-brined pork porterhouse with Coca-Cola barbeque sauce. Small plates let you taste your way around the state, and early-bird offerings in both the dining room and lounge make gourmet a good deal.

Millie's, 2603 East Main Street (804-643-5512; www.milliesdiner.com). Think gourmet diner with a global twist. Millie's is a Richmond original, and weekend brunch creates such a long line that folks bring folding chairs. Located on the east end of Main Street in Church Hill, it's not fancy, but the food has wowed the palates of national food critics from *Bon Appetit* magazine to *Southern Living*. Dinner offers the most global choices, with entrées from Thai spicy shrimp and Caribbean-spiced beef shoulder to pan-seared duck breast and grilled swordfish, but you can't go wrong with breakfast, lunch, or brunch here either.

Tail Waggers: Fido's Favorite Outings

⚏ Off-Leash Dog Parks

Barker Field at Byrd Park, 600 South Boulevard (www.richmond gov.com/parks/parkbyrd.aspx); open sunrise to sunset. Located in one of Richmond's favorite parks, the 287-acre Byrd Park near the West End, Barker Field was the city's first bark park and is still one of the most popular. The park is spread out along both sides of the boulevard and Blanton Avenue, and the dog park is located on the southern end of Blanton, near the Dogwood Dell Amphitheatre. It's usually packed with frolicking pups on the weekends.

Phideaux Field, 4401 Forest Hill Avenue, Forest Hill Presbyterian Church (804-233-4371). This is a small dog park at the church (after all, "God" is "dog" spelled backward!) and has a shorter fence than most, so if you have a jumper, this may not be the park for you. It's not worth driving across town for, but if you're in this neighborhood and Fido needs a run, it's not as crowded as the larger parks. BYOW: bring your own water to this one.

Ruff House Dog Park, 3401 Courthouse Road, Chesterfield (804-276-6661; www.ruffhousedogpark.com). Located in Rockwood Park, Ruff House is a well-maintained bark park with plenty of space for dogs to run, small and large dog enclosures, as well as water and cleanup bags. The Southside park is in the process of adding night lighting to extend play hours.

More Tail Waggers

Belle Isle, Tredegar Street (804-911-0997; www.jamesriverpark.org). Originally known as Broad Rock Island and explored by Captain John Smith, Belle Isle is an island in the James River across from the Tredegar Iron Works. During the Civil War, it was used as a prisoner-of-war camp for captured Union soldiers. Access the island by the suspension bridge beneath the Lee Bridge and you and Fido can explore the history of the island,

observe herons and other wildlife, picnic, or just enjoy the views of Hollywood Cemetery and the Richmond skyline.

Canal Walk, multiple access points at nearly every block between Fifth and 17th Streets (804-788-6466; www.venturerichmond.com); free. Canal Walk stretches for over a mile along the James River and the Kanawha and Haxall Canals. Inlaid medallions mark momentous events in the city's history, so you and your pooch can stroll and study at the same time.

History Hounds, Valentine Richmond History Center, 1015 East Clay Street (804-649-0711; http://richmondhistorycenter.com/calendar/history-hounds-oct); $10 per person; canines are free; reservations required. Throughout the year, Richmond History Center tours welcome four-legged learners to explore some of Richmond's historic neighborhoods and sites. Dogs must have current vaccinations and be leashed, and owners must bring their own supply of water and cleanup bags.

Hollywood Cemetery, 412 Cherry Street (804-648-8501; www.hollywoodcemetery.org); free. Explore this fascinating garden-style cemetery along the banks of the James River with your best friend. Three presidents are interred here: James Monroe, John Tyler, and

This cast-iron canine has guarded his family's graves since the Civil War.

Confederate President Jefferson Davis, along with thousands of Confederate soldiers and many notable Richmond residents, including Lewis Ginter. Dog lovers will enjoy one of Richmond's favorite canine legends, the Black Iron Dog. Located near the Confederate memorial, the large cast-iron pooch stands sentinel over the graves of the Reese children. According to the story, the big black dog used to be on display in front of a general store on Broad Street, and Charles Reese's children loved to stop and pet it or climb on its back. Reese finally purchased the dog statue for his children and it became a beloved family treasure, but when metals were being confiscated dur-

ing the Civil War to melt down for ammunition, the statue was moved into hiding in the cemetery, where it still stands today, once again reunited with its human family.

Lewis Ginter Botanical Garden, 1800 Lakeside Avenue (804-262-9887; www.lewisginter.org); $11. On the second Thursday of the month during the summer, the garden welcomes well-behaved, leashed dogs for its "Fidos after Five" evenings. You and your pal can stroll through the gorgeous gardens (no butterfly chasing, guys!) or just find a shady bench and enjoy the cool of the evening. There are also one or two Fido nights during the monthlong holiday Garden Fest of Lights

(Thanksgiving through New Year's), a spectacular time of year for a sparkling tour.

Monument Avenue, 2500 Monument Avenue (www.visitrich mondva.com); free. The only street in America that is designated as a National Historic Landmark, Monument Avenue is lined with historic homes and contains statues commemorating Confederate leaders like Robert E. Lee and J.E.B. Stuart, as well as one honoring Richmond native, tennis legend Arthur Ashe.

Richmond Slave Trail, Manchester Docks, Maury Street (804- 646- 7955; www.richmondgov.com/ CommissionSlaveTrail); free. Richmond was the largest source of enslaved Africans on the East Coast from 1830 to 1860. Walk in the footsteps of enslaved African Americans, following the markers on the Slave Trade Path along the James River, past the Shockoe Bottom sites of former slave auction houses, Lumpkin's Slave Jail, and the Negro Burial Ground. In 2007, the 15-foot bronze Slavery Reconciliation Statue at 15th and Main Streets was unveiled, not far from the former slave markets. The sculpture was a gesture of apology from officials in Liverpool, England, and Benin, West Africa, for their

Lewis Ginter Botanical Gardens hosts pet-friendly events throughout the summer months.

Take your pooch on a scenic history walk through Hollywood Cemetery to visit the Confederate War Memorial and the graves of Presidents James Monroe, John Tyler, and Confederate president Jefferson Davis.

roles in slave trading. Free booklets for the 1.3-mile walk are available from the city park system.

17th Street Farmers Market, 100 North 17th Street (804-646-0477; www.17thstreetfarmersmarket.com) ; free; open Saturday and Sunday 8:30 A.M. to 4:00 P.M. This historic market in Shockoe Bottom has been operating since the early 18th century. Saturday is Growers Day and Sunday adds vintage vendors to the fresh mix.

Stony Point Fashion Park, 9200 Stony Point Parkway (804-212-2660; www.shopstonypoint.com); free. This may be the most pet-friendly shopping mall in the coun-try, where many of the retail shops and boutiques display a "pets wel-come" doggy decal in their shop windows. Featuring high-end retail-ers from Louis Vuitton and Tiffany to Sur la Table and Coach, the un-enclosed mall is park-like, with fountains and benches, gardens and trees, and doggy welcome stations.

☺ Sweet Treats and Canine Chic: Where to Shop with Your BFF

Fido Park Avenue Dog Boutique, 4027 Lauderdale Drive (804-360-8011; www.fidoparkavenue.com). Inspired by New York's chic canine boutiques, Fido Park Avenue wel-comes all four-legged shoppers, and

Pet comfort stations are located throughout the open-air mall at Stony Point.

a positive-reinforcement promotion gives humans who have adopted a local shelter pet a $10 gift card. From bling to beds and everything in between—you and your pooch can find a special souvenir as you stroll the "city streets."

For the Love of Pete, 322 Libbie Avenue (804-288-3674; www.the loveofpete.com). The trendsetting stores in the Libbie/Grove corridor wouldn't forget your friend. For the Love of Pete is a local favorite for doggy duds and accessories, and if you donate a gently worn collar, you'll get a discount on a new one.

Three Dog Bakery, 9200 Stony Point Parkway (804-330-3536; www.threedogrichmond.com). Three Dog is another great reason to visit Stony Point Fashion Park, the shopping mall with a passion for pets. Pick up a Boxer Brownie or Drooly Dream Bar for your pal. All the treats are made with 100 percent human-grade ingredients.

Fido loves shopping at Stony Point in Richmond.

You!Boutiques, 11800 W Broad Street, Henrico (804-364-9686; www.youboutiques.com). If the whimsical website with the barking dog and ringing doorbell at the pet boutique door are any indication, this is a shop worth seeking out. Packed with handcrafted gifts for the pet lover, from hand-colored breed profiles to fine needlepoint pillows, hand-painted mugs, playful picture frames, and charming totes and purses, You! Pet Boutique also has lavish gifts for your four-legged friend.

Stroll down Monument Avenue with your four-legged friend to admire the grand homes and historic statues.
(Courtesy of Richmond Metropolitan Convention & Visitors Bureaus)

◉ Big-Box Stores

Petco www.petco.com, 9700 Midlothian Turnpike (804-272-1649)

PetSmart www.petsmart.com, six locations: 5515 W Broad Street (804-282-6455); 1276 Carmia Way, North Chesterfield (804-897-9490); 4531 South Laburnum Avenue (804-236-3245); 9870 Brook Road, Glen Allen (804-266-1476); 11740 West Broad Street, Short Pump (804-364-2570); 2264 Chattanooga Plaza, Midlothian (804-763-6058).

♛ A Day of Beauty: Best Pooch Primping

A Dog and Cat's World, 10823 West Broad Street (804-270-0997; www.dogsandcatsworld.com). On the far west end of town, these groomers are certified, as well as trained in pet CPR. The salon offers grooming packages and a wide range of à la carte services including teeth brushing.

The Barking Lot, 606 North Belmont Avenue (804-358-4038; http://thebarkinglot.info). This grooming salon's slogan is "Where a dirty dog is a temporary thing," and they cater to all breeds. They also have a location inside the Fin & Feather shop on Lakeside Avenue.

Crittertown Bathhouse, 2819 Hathaway Road (804-320-1096; www.crittertown.com). Located in the Stratford Hills Shopping Center,

Crittertown is a DIY dog wash that provides all your supplies and cleans up the mess when you're done!

Dogma Grooming & Pet Needs, 3501 West Cary Street (804-358-9267; http://dogmagrooming.com). This locally owned salon frequently wins "best of" awards in regional media polls. In addition to full-service grooming, Dogma carries a line of holistic and organic pet foods.

Just for Paws Pet Spa, 12341 Gayton Road (804-741-7297; www.justforpawspetspa.com). Formerly known as Groomingdales, this pet spa offers special spa packages, hydrotherapy, and pickup and drop-off service, in addition to standard grooming services. Check the website for special discounts.

Ridge Dog Shop, 1505 North Parham Road (804-288-0605; www.theridgedogshop.com). Located on the west side of the city, near Regency Square Mall, Ridge Dog Shop has been primping and pampering Richmond pooches for more than three decades.

♥ Play Dates: Doggy Daycare

All Dog Adventures, 4111 West Clay Street (804-355-7737; www.alldogadventures.com); from $30. Doggy daycare may cost more here, but pups are given a lot of one-on-one time, as well as customized socialization playtimes with no more than five other handpicked, compatible canine friends. The professional trainers here also reinforce positive behavior and offer classes in manners, agility, and tricks.

Diamond Doghouse, 1712 Ellen Road (804-254-4101; www.diamond-dog-house.com); daycare from $16; boarding from $28 per day. With spacious indoor and outdoor play areas, Diamond Doghouse also offers overnight boarding and grooming services.

Dog's Day Inn, 213 Granite Spring Road (804-745-7173; www.dogsdayinn.com); daycare from $15; boarding from $25 per day. Temperature-controlled kennels with indoor/outdoor runs and two playtimes a day, either alone or with a compatible group, and nightly "tuck-ins" with blankets and cookies for overnight guests are just some of the perks at Dog's Day Inn. Grooming services are available for both daycare dogs and boarders.

Holiday Barn, 900 Southlake Boulevard (804-794-5401; http://holidaybarn.com); from $23 per day; special packages for daycare and boarding or combined with grooming services. Promising "happy campers" and lots of "furrmazing" experiences, the Holiday Barn features doggy vacations, as well as doggy day camp. This location is on the south side of the city, but there's also one in Glen Allen in west Richmond.

Petite Pet Inn & Spa, 3010 Hilliard Road (804-622-1556; www.petite petinn.com); daycare from $20 and boarding from $30. Specializing in daycare and boarding for doggy divas 25 pounds and under, also offers grooming and spa services including massage and whirlpool therapy.

🐾 Pet Sitters

Rates begin at $12–14 per visit.

Angelic Pet Sitter Services (804-513-6479; www.angelicpetsitter services.com)

The Fan Sitter (804-475-9024; www.fansitter.com)

Love My K-9 (804-869-0488; www.lovemyk9.net)

Pet Pleasers (804-320-4395; www.pet-pleasers.com)

Worth a Sitter: Sights to See without Fido

American Civil War Center and Richmond National Battlefield and Visitor Center at Tredegar, 500 Tredegar Street (804-780-1865; www.tredegar.org); $8. Housed in the 1861 gun foundry, the American Civil War Center explores the Civil War from three perspectives: Confederate, Union, and

The Historic Tredegar Ironworks in Richmond manufactured most of the cannons used in the Civil War.

African American. It's located in the same complex as the Richmond National Battlefield at Tredegar, which is operated by the National Park Service and also has a museum, as well as Ranger-guided tours, but does not charge admission. You can easily see both on the same visit, and the Ranger tour includes Brown's Island, where ammunition was manufactured during the Civil War. Today, many of the city's concerts and festivals are held on the island. Parking is free at the Belle Island lot next door to the museum.

Berkeley Plantation, 12602 Harrison Landing Road (Route 5), Charles City (804-829-6018; www.berkeleyplantation.com); $11;

President William Henry Harrison was born at Berkeley Plantation, also the site of the first Thanksgiving celebration and where the bugle call taps was written.

(Courtesy of Richmond Metropolitan Convention & Visitors Bureau)

open daily except Thanksgiving and Christmas. This historic plantation claims to have been the site of the first Thanksgiving celebration in 1619 and is the birthplace of both Benjamin Harrison, a signer of the Declaration of Independence, and President William Henry Harrison. The taps bugle call was written here during the Civil War: Berkeley was the headquarters and supply base for McClellan's Union army.

First Friday Art Walk, (www.first fridaysrichmond.com); free. On the first Friday of the month, from 5–9 P.M., more than 40 of Richmond's galleries open their venues for an evening of browsing along Historic Broad Street, east of Belvidere

Street and west of 9th, as well as in the neighborhoods of Jackson Ward and Monroe Ward.

Historic Jackson Ward (www.hjwa .org). Nicknamed "the Harlem of the South," this neighborhood in metro Richmond has a rich history as the cultural and business center of the African American community. With more than 600 buildings listed on the National Register of Historic Places, Jackson Ward contains some of the city's architectural treasures and is said to have more decorative cast-iron work than any city outside of New Orleans. Famous residents from this neighborhood include Maggie Lena Walker (**Maggie L. Walker**

National Historic Site, www.nps .gov/mawa), the first female bank president, who founded Consolidated Bank & Trust (1st and Marshall Streets), the oldest African American–operated bank in the United States. Dance legend **Bill "Bojangles" Robinson** was also born in Jackson Ward, and a 9-foot statue at the corner of Adams and Leigh pays homage to his success. The **Black History Museum and Cultural Center of Virginia** at Clay and Foushee Streets (www.blackhistorymuseum .org) is the repository of more than 5,000 African American artifacts and continues to gather oral, visual, and written records that commemorate the lives and achievements of Virginia's African Americans.

Maymont Park, 2201 Shields Lake Drive (804-358-7166; http:// maymont.org); free; open daily 10–5. The 100-acre estate of James and Sallie Dooley includes the Victorian mansion they lived in from 1893 to 1925, a children's farm, nature center, and several spectacular gardens. While admission to the grounds is free, suggested donations for the mansion tour and nature center run from $3–5, and tours of the park via horse-drawn carriage, tram, or hay wagon are in the same price range.

Museum and White House of the Confederacy, 1201 E. Clay Street

(804-649-1861; http://moc.org). The Museum of the Confederacy houses the nation's most comprehensive collection of military, political, and domestic artifacts and art associated with the Confederacy, and offers guided tours of the White House of the Confederacy, Civil War residence of Confederate President Jefferson Davis.

Shirley Plantation, 501 Shirley Plantation Road, Charles City (804-

The White House of the Confederacy, home of Jefferson Davis, is part of the Museum of the Confederacy and is, in fact, not white at all: it's gray.

(Courtesy of Richmond Metropolitan Convention & Visitors Bureaus)

Famous Four-Legged Virginians

CIVIL WAR SALLIE

During the first month of training for the 11th Pennsylvania Volunteer Infantry Regiment, a stranger brought the captain a pug-nosed, brindled bull terrier puppy. Named after a local beauty in West Chester, Sallie became the darling of the regiment and fought alongside her human friends at Cedar Mountain, Antietam, Fredericksburg, and Chancellorsville. When Abe Lincoln reviewed the Union troops in 1863, it's said he raised his stovepipe hat to salute this canine soldier. Sallie was killed at the Battle of Hatcher's Run in Stafford, Virginia, on February 6, 1865, and even though her regiment was under heavy fire, her friends stopped to bury her on the battlefield. Many years later, the survivors of the 11th PA Regiment dedicated a monument on the Gettysburg Battlefield: a bronze soldier atop a marble pedestal. But if you look closely at the front of the monument, you'll see a small bronze dog at the soldier's feet. Sallie still watches over her men as she did during all those battles, and the men she befriended made sure that she, too, would be remembered for her love, loyalty, and sacrifice (http://nycivilwar.us/sallie.html).

829-5121; www.shirleyplantation.com); $11; open daily except Thanksgiving and Christmas. Founded in 1613, Shirley is Virginia's first plantation and is still owned and operated by the eleventh generation of the family, making it also the oldest family-owned business in North America. Still a working plantation and private home, Shirley is one of the most intact 18th-century estates in the state. The house is furnished with original paintings, woodwork, and silver of the Hill Carter family and has some unique architectural features like the "flying staircase" and the Queen Anne forecourt. During the Civil War, after the Battle of Malvern Hill in 1862,

Union troops descended on the plantation with their wounded. The compassionate care given to the soldiers by the women of Shirley compelled Union General McClellan to grant the plantation a written exemption, saving it from being burned and looted.

St. John's Church Reenactment, 2401 E. Broad Street (804-648-5015; http://historicstjohns church.org); free on summer Sundays at 2 P.M. Built in 1741, St. John's is the oldest wooden church in Virginia and still has an active congregation. In 1775, Patrick Henry gave his fiery "Give me liberty or give me death" speech here, and on Sunday

Patrick Henry gave his famous "Give me liberty or give me death" speech at St. John's Church in Church Hill. You can see a reenactment of the rousing speech on Sundays.

afternoons during the summer, professional actors perform a reenactment of that debate between 10 of the nation's founding fathers.

Valentine Richmond History Center, 1015 E. Clay Street (804-649-0711; http://richmondhistory center.com); $8 one-day admission includes Valentine Richmond History Center exhibition galleries, the Edward V. Valentine Sculpture Studio, and the Wickham House (1812); $10 Court End pass includes all of those plus the John Marshall House and the Black History Museum and Cultural Center of Virginia and is valid for one year. Over 400 years of Richmond's history is reflected in the museum exhibits and the two historic houses

included in the Court End pass. Richmond History Tours, both guided bus tours and walking tours, also depart from the center.

Virginia Capitol and Executive Mansion, 1000 Bank Street (visitor entrance at 10th and Bank) (804-698-1788; www.virginiacapitol .gov); free; Monday through Saturday 8:00 A.M. to 5:00 P.M. and Sundays from 1:00 P.M. to 5:00 P.M. Designed by Thomas Jefferson, the Capitol has been home to the General Assembly since 1788. Not only is the state assembly the oldest continuously operating legislature in the Western Hemisphere, the building itself was the first in America in the monumental classical style. You can take either a self-

This statue of George Washington, one of eight presidents from Virginia, stands in the Rotunda of the State Capitol. (Courtesy of Richmond Metropolitan Convention & Visitors Bureaus)

guided or guided tour of both the historic 18th-century Old Capitol building with its grand Rotunda filled with paintings and statues of Virginia's eight presidents (the reason the state is known as the Mother of Presidents), as well as the modern working spaces of the current state government. Take a few minutes to browse the gift shop or grab a bite to eat at Meriwether's Café, both located off the main hall near the visitors' entrance. If you want to see the state government in action, there is a public gallery for viewing during sessions, but space is limited.

Virginia Museum of Fine Arts, 200 North Boulevard (804-340-1580; www.vmfa.state.va.us); free general admission for permanent collections; open daily, 365 days a year. After a multimillion-dollar renovation and expansion, VMFA is one of the premier art museums in the nation. With more than 23,000 works of art from every major culture in the world, the museum has stunning collections of art nouveau, art deco, modern and contemporary American art, as well as French impressionist and postimpressionist art, British sporting art, and a world-renowned collection of Fabergé jeweled objects. Take a lunch break at the Best Café overlooking the Sculpture Garden or splurge on dinner at the Amuse Restaurant.

Charlottesville: Jefferson's Virginia

Native Virginian George Washington may be the father of our country and our first president, but to many Virginians, Thomas Jefferson is the father of the Old Dominion. This is especially true in Charlottesville, the cultural heart of central Virginia, nestled in the foothills of the Blue Ridge Mountains, where residents refer to the region as Jefferson's Virginia.

While the Renaissance man's architectural genius is reflected throughout the state, his hilltop home, Monticello, and the University of Virginia, which he founded at the age of 76, are gems in his architectural portfolio. It was here that Jefferson introduced European vinifera to America, and although

(Continued on page 119)

An early-morning stroll with the Keswick Hall hounds. (Courtesy of Keswick Hall at Monticello)

Fido 411

Here are some of the most important numbers to have when you arrive in Charlottesville:

✚ 24-hour Emergency Veterinarians

Greenbrier Emergency Animal Hospital, 370 Greenbrier Drive (434-202-1616; www.greenbrier-emergency.com). One of the newest animal hospitals in the region, Greenbrier is open from 6 P.M. to 8 A.M. Monday to Friday, and 24 hours on weekend days, including major holidays.

Veterinary Emergency Treatment Service & Specialty (VETSS), 1540 Airport Road (434-973-3519; http://emergency-vets.com). VETSS is open 24/7, 365 days a year for emergency and critical care services in the Charlottesville area.

Animal Poison Control Center—ASPCA (888-426-4435 or www.aspca .org/pet-care/poison-control/). If you think your pet may have ingested a poisonous substance or animal, help is available 24 hours a day, 365 days a year.

To find an emergency care veterinarian from your smartphone, check the following websites for the closest location:

www.vetsnearyou.com, **www .localvets.com**, or **www.animal clinicsnearyou.com** Enter the zip code of your location and it will bring up a list and map of the closest veterinarians.

24-hour Pharmacies

To find a 24-hour pharmacy, check the store-locator search on one of these websites:

CVS: www.cvs.com

Walgreens: www.walgreens.com

RX List: www.rxlist.com/ pharmacy/local_locations_pharmacies.htm

Travel 411

While Charlottesville is beautiful in the fall, the town is packed to capacity on University of Virginia home football weekends. Similarly, attractions like Monticello have long waiting lines during peak travel times. Driving through the mountains, especially around Afton, can be treacherous in heavy fog or inclement weather.

D-Tails

Charlottesville Convention & Visitors Bureau www.visitcharlottesville .org

Monticello www.monticello.org

Humans and their four-legged friends shop on Charlottesville's pedestrian mall.

his own vineyards were never successful, his legacy has flourished. In this region alone, the Monticello American Viticultural Area (AVA) produces some of the state's best vintages. Fittingly, Virginia winemaker and Monticello's Assistant Director of Gardens and Grounds, Gabriele Rausse, often called the father of Virginia wine for his contributions to many of the Old Dominion's premier vineyards in Virginia's early years of viticulture, is carrying out Jefferson's vision at Monticello today, as well as overseeing his own boutique vineyard.

In addition to being a statesman, the principal writer of the Declaration of Independence, and our third president, Jefferson was also a passionate farmer and gardener, with a scientific mind that loved solving problems. His 1,000-foot terrace garden could be called the first farm-to-table dining experience, and his experiments with over 250 species of vegetables, including

Monticello Wine Trail

In 2012, *Wine Enthusiast* magazine named Virginia one of the world's 10 best wine destinations. With more than 200 wineries throughout the state, Virginia is the fifth-largest wine producer in America, and many of its finest vineyards are located in the Monticello American Viticultural Area (AVA), where Thomas Jefferson's vision of producing wines in his native state rivaling those of the Old World has finally come to fruition. Virginia's signature wine is Viognier, a grape originally from France's Rhône Valley, that does particularly well in this region.

Many of the 25 vineyards on the Monticello Wine Trail (www.monticello winetrail.com) are pet friendly, but call ahead for specific policies. In most cases, you can tour the vineyards with your four-legged friend, but not every winery allows Fido in the tasting room, so oenophiles may want to get a sitter. Tastings are usually in the $5–8 range and many of the wineries are open seven days a week (check websites for hours). If you don't have time to do the entire trail, here are a few highlights:

Barboursville Vineyards, 17655 Winery Road, Barboursville (540-832-3824; www.barboursvillewine.com). Located in Orange County, this award-winning winery draws more visitors annually than the nearby home of President James Madison (Montpelier) and is known for its stellar Bordeaux-like red, Octagon, as well as for its Viognier. On the property are historic ruins of the Barbour estate house, designed by Thomas Jefferson, as well as another family villa that is now an inn. If you don't have your four-legged friend with you, have lunch or dinner at the lovely Palladio Restaurant, specializing in northern Italian cuisine. The restaurant also hosts special wine dinners and cooking classes.

Blenheim Vineyards, 31 Blenheim Farm, Charlottesville (434-293-5366; www.blenheimvineyards.com). Owner Dave Matthews may be more well known for making music than wine, but this vineyard has made great strides in just a decade. Try his rock-star red, the Petit Verdot.

DelFosse Vineyards & Winery, 500 DelFosse Winery Lane, Faber (434-263-6100; www.delfossewine.com). DelFosse is known for its Petit Verdot and Viognier. One of the coolest things about this vineyard is its pet-friendly log cabin for overnight stays, where you have your own wine bar on the deck overlooking the vineyards

Flying Fox Vineyards, 27 Chapel Hollow Road, Afton (434-361-1692; www.FlyingFoxVineyard.com). Local wine aficionados rave about the Cabernet Franc and Petit Verdot from this friendly, low-key boutique vineyard. Given Flying Fox's limited production, if you find something you like, buy multiples, since it's sure to sell out quickly.

Barboursville is one of the most popular wineries in Virginia, drawing more visitors than President James Madison's home, Montpelier, which is nearby. (Courtesy of Barboursville Vineyards)

Horton Cellars Winery, 6399 Spotswood Trail, Gordonsville (540-832-7440; www.hvwine.com). Horton is all about the whites: its Viognier is recommended by the head of the American Sommelier Association and its Petit Manseng is a must-try.

Jefferson Vineyards, 1353 Thomas Jefferson Parkway, Charlottesville (434-977-3042; www.jefferson vineyards.com). Located on one of Thomas Jefferson's original 1774 vineyard sites close to Monticello, Jefferson Vineyards offers a taste of history along with award-winning Cabernet Franc, Meritage, and Pinot Gris. Jefferson's first plantings of European vinifera varietals was a dismal failure, and more than 200 years passed before this vineyard was reborn.

Keswick Vineyards, 1575 Keswick Winery Drive, Keswick (434-244-3341; www.keswickvineyards.com). Dogs are always welcome here, both on the grounds and in the tasting room, but if your pal likes to socialize, try to catch Yappy Hour on Sunday afternoons in the picnic area. A portion of the proceeds from every bottle of wine sold during that time goes to a local shelter, so pick up a bottle or two of Keswick's award-winning Viognier or unique Verdejo.

Prince Michel Vineyards & Winery, 154 Winery Lane, Leon (540-547-3707; www.princemichel.com). Winner of *Virginia Wine Lover Magazine*'s Visitor's Choice Award, Prince Michel is a beautiful property, popular for destination weddings and special events. Friendly and well-behaved Fidos are even allowed in the tasting room, and if you've ever wanted your own custom-label wine, Prince Michel is the place to get it: they specialize in custom labels for anniversaries and special events.

Veritas Vineyards & Winery, 145 Saddleback Farm Road, Afton (540-456-8000; www.veritaswines.com). Located at the foot of the Blue Ridge Mountains, Veritas uses Old World principles combined with modern technology to produce its wines. Leashed pets are welcome on the grounds, but not in the tasting room. Take turns and definitely try the Viognier.

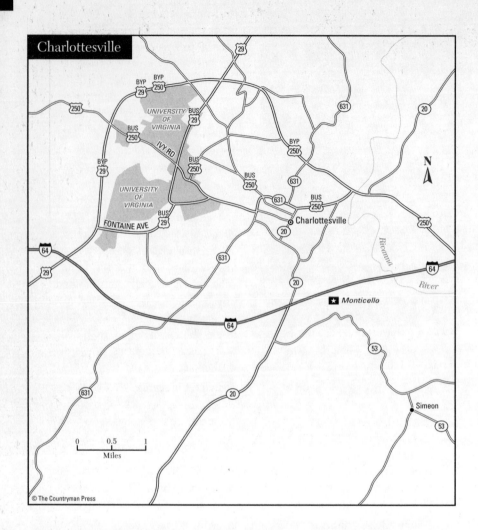

Charlottesville

© The Countryman Press

figs from France and squash from Italy, may also be part of the reason he is often also credited with being the father of American gastronomy.

Today, Charlottesville is still the cultural capital of central Virginia, reflecting many of Jefferson's passions, from verdant vineyards and fine dining to education, art, and music. The rolling hills of the Piedmont are 70 miles northwest of Richmond off I-64, and although it's easy to get around the city itself on foot or using the free trolley service, you'll need a car to explore the presidential homes, wineries, and historic attractions in the region. Welcome at elegant country inns, wineries, and on Charlottesville's pet-friendly downtown pedestrian mall, you and your four-legged friend can celebrate your independence in true Jeffersonian style.

Best Beds: Comfy Sleeps For You and Your Canine Family

DoubleTree by Hilton, 990 Hilton Heights Road, Charlottesville (434-973-2121; www.doubletree.hilton .com); from $139 per night. Located about 4 miles from the University of Virginia near the airport, the DoubleTree welcomes pets 30 pounds and under with a one-time, nonrefundable fee of $25. While this 235-room hotel may not have the Federal charm of other area resorts and hotels, it has all the modern amenities you would expect from the Hilton family.

Keswick Hall at Monticello, 701 Club Drive, Keswick (434-979-3440; www.keswick.com); from $225 per night. This 1912 Tuscan villa on 600 lush acres a few miles east of Charlottesville was named the #1 Top Small Resort, USA Mainland, by *Condé Nast Traveler*. Offering refined elegance that Thomas Jefferson would surely have approved of, Keswick has 48 opulent rooms and suites furnished with English and American antiques, as well as modern and luxurious amenities. There's no formal check-in desk here; you'll be welcomed as if you were a private guest at this mansion, and Fido is considered to

Join local members of the Keswick Club for a round of golf. (Courtesy of Keswick Hall at Monticello)

You and Fido can live a life of country elegance at Keswick Hall.

(Courtesy of Keswick Hall at Monticello)

be a member of the family too. Pampered-pooch amenities include a welcome treat, a comfy bed, and food and water bowls in your room. The chef will prepare special canine meals upon request, and pet-sitting services are also available if you want to explore the area or play a round on the 18-hole, Arnold Palmer course at the resort. Well-mannered dogs under 75 pounds are welcome with a onetime $75 nonrefundable cleaning fee. The resort is owned by the same group that owns the five-star Jefferson Hotel in Richmond, so if you're planning to visit both areas, packages are available that include both the resort and the hotel.

The Clifton Inn, 1296 Clifton Drive, Charlottesville (434-971-1800; www.cliftoninn.net); from $195 per night. A member of the Relais & Chateaux group, this quaint country inn set on 100 acres exemplifies luxury living in a rural and historic setting. The property has ties to the Jefferson family, once owned by Thomas Jefferson's daughter and her husband, Thomas Mann. In fact, the foundations of the main building are thought to be the original foundations of one of Mann's warehouses. With just 18 exquisitely appointed rooms and suites and refined amenities like Mascioni linens, you wouldn't expect the inn to be pet friendly.

However, 11 rooms (exceptions are rooms in the main house) welcome your canine companion with no restrictions and a onetime $75 fee per stay. Walk your pal around the grounds and private lake to work off your complimentary daily afternoon tea. The inn's restaurant is a destination on its own, offering a wonderful seasonal tasting menu.

The Mark Addy Inn, 56 Rodes Farm Drive, Nellysford (434-361-1101; www.mark-addy.com); from $159 per night. This beautifully restored Victorian has a rich history, located on the site of what was once called Upland Manor, a weekend sporting retreat for Charles Everett and his friend, Thomas Jefferson. Featuring pet-friendly information on their home page and a house dog named Coalby, this pet-friendly B&B offers amenities for four-legged guests including beds, bowls, and treats. Onetime pet fees are based on weight: $25 for up to 15 pounds, $40 for up to 40 pounds, and $50 for canines over 40 pounds (there are some breed restrictions, so check with the inn before booking). The inn's dining outlet, the Fountain Room, serves breakfast and dinner, and its international cuisine, accompanied by a fine list of Virginia wines, often draws locals for the dinner

Coalby, the canine innkeeper at the Mark Addy Inn, was included in the wedding festivities when his human, Jennie, got married. (Courtesy of the Mark Addy Inn)

Famous Four-Legged Virginians

KESWICK'S FAVORITE FURRY EMPLOYEE

Wendy, a border collie, has worked and lived at Keswick Hall for the past ten years. Formerly the pet of a retired couple, Wendy needed a job (border collies are natural herders), so Keswick Hall purchased the precocious pup and put her to work. She rides the golf course with Keswick club superintendent Pete McDonough and chases geese off the course. Members of the club and guests at Keswick Hall love visiting with the canine "geese police officer"!

Wendy chases geese from the golf course at the Keswick Club.

(Courtesy of Keswick Hall at Monticello)

seating, so be sure to make a reservation. Guests of the inn get a hot, three-course breakfast included in the room rate.

Omni Charlottesville, 235 West Main Street, Charlottesville (434-971-5500; www.omnihotels.com); from $179 per night. If you want to stay in town, within walking distance of most of the shops, restaurants, and nightclubs, the Omni is all about location. The triangular hotel anchors one end of the pedestrian mall, so you're literally steps from the action. Pets 25 pounds and under are welcome with a non-refundable $50 cleaning fee per stay.

Best Bowls: Restaurants Worth a Sitter

NOTE: In true Jeffersonian spirit, restaurateurs in Charlottesville embrace the farm-to-table movement wholeheartedly, sourcing their food from local and sustainable purveyors so many menus change daily.

Brookville, 225 West Main Street (434-202-2791; www.brookville restaurant.com; closed Monday). This neighborhood favorite features down-home food like Virginia ham fritters and Surry sausage alongside artisanal cheeses from around the globe. Chef-owner Harrison Keevil puts a modern twist on the classic techniques he learned at the French Culinary Institute and as an apprentice of regional superstar Chef Dean Maupin.

Clifton Inn, 1296 Clifton Inn Drive (434-971-1800; www.cliftoninn .net). Foodies will want to sit at the unique eight-seat chef's counter so they can pepper the culinary pros with questions as they watch their multicourse menu unfold. If you prefer alfresco dining, the terrace is lovely, or you can opt for the formality of the dining room. Rather than a static menu, you choose from seasonal options to create your own palate-pleasing menu.

Fossett's at Keswick Hall, 701 Club View Drive, Keswick (434-979-3440; www.keswick.com). You'll need to dress for dinner at this Tuscan villa set in the gorgeous Charlottesville countryside (no jeans or shorts; jackets recommended), but it will be well worth it and you'll feel right at home in this impressive mansion. With floor-to-ceiling windows that overlook the estate, and a romantic terrace for alfresco dining, Fossett's is named for Thomas Jefferson's chief cook, Edith Fossett, who mastered the art of French cooking to please the great man's adventurous palate. Fossett's pays homage to both the man and the French classics with an innovative seasonal menu that

Jefferson would love: warm duck confit salad, buffalo carpaccio, potato-crusted Shenandoah Valley trout, and Mount Vernon Farms lamb loin are just a few examples. To experience a wide array of regional favorites, try the chef's tasting menu.

Hamilton's, 101 West Main Street (434-295-6649; www.hamiltons restaurant.com; closed Sunday). Open for lunch and dinner six days a week (reservations recommended for both) and lauded by *Southern Living* magazine for its elegance, even Hamilton's classic offerings like grilled tenderloin have a Southern twist: in this case, whiskey-pecan butter. Their vegetarian "blue plate special" is sure to be a dazzling array of the best seasonal produce in the region.

Old Mill Room at the Boar's Head, 200 Ednam Drive (434-972-2230; www.boarsheadinn.com). Built from the abandoned timbers of an old gristmill, this AAA four-diamond restaurant (for 24 consecutive years) at the Boar's Head inn is a local favorite for holidays and special occasions. Expect fine dining classics from pan-seared foie gras and lobster bisque to beef and pork tenderloin and a variety of sustainable seafood. Stellar service and an excellent wine list, along with the rustic ambience, encourage guests to linger.

Tail Waggers: Fido's Favorite Outings

⠿ Dog Parks

Azalea Park, Old Lynchburg Road and I-64 (www.charlottesville.org); open 6 A.M. to 9 P.M. This 23-acre park has a fenced area for off-leash play and a bag dispenser for cleanup. Pets must be leashed in other areas of the park.

Chris Greene Lake Park, 4748 Chris Greene Lake Road (www .albemarle.org); open 7 A.M. to dusk daily. You can swim with your pooch in the special roped-off water area, or play ball in the one-acre fenced-off leash area. The dog park is located near the main parking area for the beach: at the top of the lot, you'll see the dog park sign and trail to access it.

Darden Towe Park, 445 Darden Towe Park Road (www.albemarle .org); open 7 A.M. to dusk daily. Located past the picnic shelter, the dog park is a one-acre enclosed off-leash play area.

⠿ More Tail Waggers

Blue Mountain Brewery, 9519 Critzer's Shop Road, Afton (540-456-8020; www.bluemountain brewery.com). Located about 20 miles from Charlottesville, the Blue Ridge Mountain Brewery crafts ales and lagers with the pure waters of the mountains, served up with hearty, homemade fare from pretzels to beer-boiled bratwurst. Take

The Blue Mountain Brewery welcomes canine visitors . . . no ID required!

(Courtesy of the Blue Mountain Brewery)

Adah Alfano picked up a floppy-eared hat from one of the many street vendors on the mall.

a break with your four-legged pal on one of two patios and cool off with a Full Nelson Pale Ale or Blue Mountain Lager.

Carter Mountain Orchard, 1435 Carters Mountain Trail, Charlottesville (434-977-1833; www.cartermountainorchard.com); open Monday to Saturday 9–6, Sunday 10–5; four-legged visitors must be leashed. You and your pooch can pick your own apples or peaches at this historic orchard or just pick up a bushel to take home. Just minutes from Monticello, the orchard was part of a 9,350-acre land grant obtained by John Carter, Esquire, in 1729 that included what

is still called Carter Mountain. Carter was the secretary of the Colony of Virginia, and the Carter family is one of the oldest and most influential in the history of Colonial Virginia.

Charlottesville Downtown Mall, Main Street, Charlottesville (www.downtowncharlottesville .net). The six-block pedestrian mall is packed with specialty stores, galleries, restaurants, and coffeehouses in restored 19th- and 20th-century buildings. Think of it as a dog park with window shopping! You'll meet a lot of local four-legged residents out for a stroll.

The restaurant at the Clifton Inn has a counter where you can interact with the chefs while they're preparing your gourmet meal. (Courtesy of the Clifton Inn)

Charlottesville City Market, corner of Water and South Streets (434-970-3371; www.charlottesville citymarket.com). Every Saturday from 7 A.M. to noon from April through December, the City Market offers local produce, arts and crafts, and a wide variety of foodstuffs. In December, this becomes the Christmas Market, full of decorations and gift items.

Keswick Vineyards Yappy Hour, 1575 Keswick Winery Drive, Keswick (434-244-3341; www .keswickvineyards.com). Every Sunday from the beginning of April to the end of October, Keswick hosts a Yappy Hour to benefit local animal-rescue groups. You and your pal are both allowed in the tasting room, but Keswick also offers outdoor tastings so your pooch can socialize while you sip. A portion of the purchase price of each bottle of wine sold that day goes to the local groups.

University of Virginia, Central Grounds Parking Garage, 400 Emmet Street South (434-924-7969; www .virginia.edu). Referred to simply as "the University" by locals, Thomas Jefferson's educational and architectural contribution to the state is a wonderful place for you and your pal to see the blending of the old and the new. Explore the green, terraced Lawn surrounded by redbrick buildings, and walk by the Rotunda, Jefferson's half-scale replica of Rome's Pantheon. Note that home football weekends in the fall draw crowds and are not a good time to explore the campus.

Wild Wolf Brewery, 2461 Rockfish Valley Highway, Nellysford (434-361-0088; www.wildwolfbeer.com). You're invited to "bring your growler," pull up a seat on the deck, and savor an Alpha Ale at this canine-centric brewery. Serving lunch and Sunday brunch, Wild Wolf pays homage to the species with Wolf Pack Nachos and Wild Dawgs (hot dogs), but also honors noncarnivores with selections like the vegan chipotle bean burger. In the mood for dessert? Try a signature Strawberry Schwarzcake brew.

☻ Sweet Treats and Canine Chic: Where to Shop with Your BFF

Dog and Horse Lovers Boutique, 503 East Main Street (434-220-4540; www.dogandhorse.com). The owner's German shepherd, Tyler, put his paw print of approval on the all-natural, homemade doggy treats sold at the shop, while their horses, Fancy and Baron, taste-tested the horse treats, made with shredded carrots and apples. The boutique also offers a variety of dog- and horse-themed apparel, all kinds of accessories for both kinds of four-legged friends, and welcomes Fido to come in for a treat or

Try an Alpha Ale at the Wild Wolf Brewery.   (Courtesy of Wild Wolf Brewery)

Delfosse Delight: No Whining, Just Wining

Stay in a pet-friendly historic chestnut log cabin in the middle of Delfosse Vineyards. What was once the original tasting room is now a cozy country retreat overlooking the lake, vineyards, and winery. You and your pal can cozy up in front of the fireplace or enjoy a private wine tasting at your own wine bar on the deck. The cabin has a full kitchen, as well as satellite television and Wi-Fi if you want to settle in for a week or more (www. www.delfossewine.com /escape.htm).

a try-on. The shop also carries several locally made and eco-friendly pet products.

Big-Box Stores

Petco www.petco.com, 621 Emmet Street North (434-244-6338)

PetSmart www.petsmart.com, 101 Community Street (434-964-9213)

Pet Supplies Plus www.petsupplies plus.com, 240 Seminole Trail (434-979-2009)

A Day of Beauty: Best Pooch Primping

Dirty Dogs, 22 Rio Road West (434-964-9274; www.dirtydogsdogwash .com). This DIY doggy wash says "You bring the dog, we supply the

rest," and they do. With four private washrooms that have elevated, walk-up tubs, waterproof aprons, a variety of shampoos and towels and dryers, Dirty Dogs is ready whenever your pooch needs a canine cleaning.

Pantops Pet Salon & Spa, 504 Pantops Center (434-293-2424; http://pantopspetsalon.com/). This doggy day spa specializes in canine clips, baths, and therapeutic treatments for pooches of all sizes, using hand scissoring and shaping techniques worthy of a show dog.

NOTE: Many of the daycare and boarding facilities, as well as the big-box pet stores listed in this chapter {true in all chapters}, also offer à la carte grooming services.

Play Dates: Doggy Daycare

The Dogg House, 2101 Berkmar Drive (434-975-DOGS; www.the dogghouse.com); from $18. Offering boarding and grooming services, the Dogg House prides itself on PPA: Pet Personal Attention. Doggy suites range in size from "penthouse" for pocketbook pooches to "presidential suites" for canines topping 100 pounds. All accommodations have an outdoor patio, although your pal also gets two "business" breaks a day included in the rate. You can schedule individual outdoor playtime sessions or urban walks for a small additional fee.

Pampered Pets, 601 Concord Avenue (434-293-7387; www .pamperedpetscville.com); daycare from $12; boarding from $17 per night. Offering day camp, full-service boarding, and grooming, Pampered Pets has both indoor and outdoor play areas, and all pets get one-on-one attention throughout their stay. Boarders get an afternoon ice cream treat and a special treat again at bedtime, and you can add on special playtime activities, from an individual walk to a game of Frisbee or some special cuddling time. Day camp is supervised by a certified trainer, and all counselors are certified in pet first aid. If your dog just needs a day of beauty, there's also a pet salon on site.

The Pet Motel and Salon, 187 5th Street (434-295-3679; http://pet motelandsalon.com/); from $20. This is an indoor boarding kennel, although there is an outdoor exercise area and pets are taken out three times a day. Each kennel contains a platform bed for sleeping, but does not have any outside run area, so this may not be an ideal situation for a high-energy dog, but would be fine for a senior pet or for a short stay while you explore the sights. Grooming services are also available.

Wakefield Kennel, 800 Earlysville Forest Drive, Earlysville (434-973-5171; www.wakefieldkennel.com); from $19. A few miles outside Charlottesville, Wakefield Kennel has been owned by the same family for over 30 years. The country setting and huge outdoor play areas, along with a range of special services like nature walks, may be especially attractive for large dogs and active canines. Play areas are 40-foot-square fenced enclosures with plenty of running room, and special walks in the fields and wooded areas can be arranged for an additional fee.

Worth a Sitter: Sights to See without Fido

NOTE: The Presidents' Pass will save you $5 on the individual admission prices to Monticello, Ash Lawn-Highland and Michie Tavern. You can purchase it online at www.monticello.org or at any of the three attractions.

Ash Lawn–Highland, 2050 James Monroe Parkway, also known as SR795 (434-293-8000; www.ash lawnhighland.org); $12 or included in the Presidents' Pass $40 (also Monticello and Michie Tavern); open April to October 9–6, November to March 11–5. Built in 1799, just 2 miles from the grand home of his friend Thomas Jefferson, James Monroe's residence is a simple Colonial farmhouse. The estate was originally known as Highland, and was bequeathed in 1974 to the College of William & Mary (Monroe's alma mater) by Jay

Winston and Helen Lambert Johns. Today, the historic house is a museum, packed with gifts from notables from Monroe's service as an envoy to France, Spain, and Britain. The unassuming statesman began his 50-year-long career as a public servant in 1782 with his election to the Virginia General Assembly. He served as President James Madison's secretary of state and secretary of war during the War of 1812 and was elected president in 1816. The estate includes a 535-acre working farm.

Michie Tavern, 683 Thomas Jefferson Parkway (434-977-1234; www.michietavern.com); $9 or $7 with lunch; Presidents' Pass $40 includes the tavern tour, Ash Lawn–Highland, and Monticello. The 18th-century tavern built in 1784, an example of the architecture of the Colonial Revival period, was moved to its present location close to Monticello in 1927. The tavern tour is interactive, with demonstrations of period games including Shut the Box and the Alphabet Game.

Monticello, 931 Thomas Jefferson Parkway, also known as SR53 (434-984-9822; www.monticello.org); $24 March to October, $17 November to February; open daily except Christmas; see website for seasonal hours. Aside from the sheer grandeur of Thomas Jefferson's mountaintop home

(Monticello means "little mountain"), the most intriguing furnishings in the house are Jefferson's inventions: a seven-day clock and the first robo-signer, a machine with two pens that allowed him to copy his correspondence as he was writing. Jefferson was an amateur botanist as well, and his gardens have been re-created, including the 1,000-foot terrace garden with more than 300 varieties of vegetables from around the world, and fruit orchards with 170 varieties of peaches, apples, and grapes. Jefferson introduced European vinifera to the New World, and while his vineyards weren't successful, today wines are being produced on those same tracts. Named Mulberry Row for the trees planted along it, the heart and soul of Jefferson's plantation were the slaves who worked it. Their history, along with their slave quarters and work areas, is also displayed and interpreted in the context of their origins. Jefferson died on July 4th, and it is fitting that on that date, new American citizens take their oath at Monticello. One of the most visited historic sites in Virginia, Monticello is always busy, but try to visit on a weekday when lines will be shorter.

Montpelier, 11407 Constitution Highway, also known as SR20 (540-672-2728; www.montpelier .org); $18; open daily except

Thanksgiving and Christmas; see website for seasonal hours. About a 30-minute drive from Charlottesville, Montpelier was the lifelong residence of the fourth American president, James Madison. He grew up here and retired here with his wife, Dolley, after his term of office. The DuPont family eventually purchased the estate, and in her will, Marion duPont Scott left the property to the National Trust for Historic Preservation, with the stipulation that it be restored to its original state, a project that took several years and $24 million. Included in the admission ticket are a guided tour of the Madison home, admission to the 2,650-acre gardens and grounds, the Gilmore Cabin, the William duPont Gallery, the family and slave cemeteries, and the active archaeological digs. Montpelier is also the home of the Montpelier Hunt Races, a steeplechase held on the first Saturday of November that has become one of Virginia's signature annual events since its inception in 1929. Known as the First

Lady of Racing, Marion DuPont Scott created the steeplechase and was also instrumental in the development of Virginia's top equine medical center in Leesburg, which is named in her honor.

Rotunda Tour at UVA, 1717 University Avenue or Central Grounds Parking Garage, 400 Emmet Street South (434-924-7969; www.virginia.edu); free. Tours of Thomas Jefferson's Rotunda, a half-scale replica of Rome's Pantheon and a design that also influenced Monticello and the US Capitol, are held daily at 10, 11, 2, 3, and 4 beginning on the lower level of the Lawn side. Former UVA student Edgar Allan Poe's room is preserved on the West Range. Jefferson called UVA "the hobby of my old age," founding the school at the age of 76. There are no tours during the December holiday break or in May prior to graduation. The Charlottesville Area Transit Authority (CAT) offers a free trolley service daily between downtown and the University.

Following in George Washington's Footsteps: Historic Alexandria, Fredericksburg, and the Northern Neck

Just 6 miles south of Washington, DC, the independent city of Alexandria was once a part of the nation's capital. Founded in 1749, the city grew up around what is now called Old Town, nestled on the western bank of the Potomac River. Alexandria was a major Colonial seaport and slave trading port, and notables from George Washington to Robert E. Lee called the city home. Thomas Jefferson, along with Washington and Lee, entertained friends and talked politics at Gadsby's Tavern, still welcoming travelers and local residents today. The 250-year-old brick paved streets of Old Town are lined with wonderful examples of 18th- and 19th-century architecture and filled with

(Continued on page 139)

Civil War reenactors in Fredericksburg fire a canon during the heat of battle.

(Courtesy of Fredericksburg Area Tourism)

Fido 411

Here are some of the most important numbers to have when you arrive in Alexandria, Fredericksburg and the Northern Neck:

✚ 24-hour Emergency Veterinarians

VCA Animal Hospital, 2660 Duke Street, Alexandria (703-823-3601; www.vcahospitals.com/alexandria). Open 24/7, 365 days a year, this is the closest emergency facility to Historic Old Town Alexandria.

Animal Emergency Clinic of Fredericksburg, 1210 Snowden Street, Fredericksburg (540-371-0554; www.aecfred.com). Providing critical emergency services, AEC is open from 6 P.M. to 8 A.M. Monday through Friday and from 12 P.M. Saturday to 8 A.M. Monday.

NOTE: The Northern Neck is a rural area and has no 24-hour veterinary emergency clinics, although some local veterinarians do provide cell phone numbers on their after-hours recordings. Depending on your location, you may be referred to either Fredericksburg or Peninsula Veterinary Emergency in Yorktown (see Fido 411 in the Historic Triangle chapter).

Animal Poison Control Center—ASPCA, (888-426-4435 or www.aspca .org/pet-care/poison-control/). If you think your pet may have ingested a poisonous substance or animal, help is available 24 hours a day, 365 days a year.

To find an emergency-care veterinarian from your smartphone, check the following websites for the closest location:

www.vetsnearyou.com, www.localvets.com, or **www.animalclinic snearyou.com** Enter the zip code of your location and it will bring up a list and map of the closest veterinarians.

◗ 24-hour Pharmacies

To find a 24-hour pharmacy, check the store-locator search on one of these websites:

CVS: www.cvs.com

Walgreens: www.walgreens.com

RX List: www.rxlist.com/pharmacy/local_locations_pharmacies.htm

D-Tails

Visit Alexandria www.visitalexandria.com

Visit Fairfax County www.fxva.com

Visit Fredericksburg www.visitfred.com

Visit the Northern Neck www.northernneck.org

Travel 411

Fredericksburg and the Northern Neck are an easy drive from Richmond or from Northern Virginia. You'll need at least two days to explore Alexandria and the surrounding areas, so plan a stopover in Northern Virginia. All three locations have excellent pet-friendly accommodations, although the number of rooms are limited in Fredericksburg and the Northern Neck, and Alexandria will be packed during the summer season, so reserve in advance. The Northern Neck is rural, with few specialty pet stores or services, so be sure to pack your pet's medications, any special high-end or raw foods (stores on the Northern Neck are general grocery and discount chains), and also take a pet first aid kit.

exclusive boutiques and restaurants, combining the urban sophistication of the neighboring nation's capital with the Colonial charm of our forefathers.

While there is much more to the city than Old Town, most of the historic attractions are centered in this area. George Washington's most famous home, Mount Vernon, is 8 miles south of Old Town at the southern end of the George Washington Memorial Parkway. If you head north on the parkway (which has access to Duke Street entering Old Town), it's also about 8 miles

Gadsby's Tavern in Old Town Alexandria has been serving good food since 1770 and was a favorite of George Washington. (Alexandria Convention & Visitors Association)

How Stonewall Jackson Got His Nickname at the First Battle of the Civil War

The first major land battle of the Civil War was fought in Prince William County near the city of Manassas. Called the First Battle of Bull Run (and also known as First Manassas), Union forces led by General Irvin McDowell planned to march on Richmond and put an early end to the rebellious Confederacy. At Manassas Junction, the Confederate Army under the command of General Beauregard initially floundered in the fight, but reinforcements from the Shenandoah Valley arrived by train to save the day. The brigade of Virginians was under the command of Colonel Thomas J. Jackson, a former instructor at the Virginia Military Institute. Jackson's band stood their ground and the fierce battle turned into a rout, with the Union forces fleeing. From then on, Jackson was known as Stonewall Jackson. In August 1862, the two armies again clashed on the battlefield at Manassas, with the Confederate Army victorious.

Manassas National Battlefield Park, 6511 Sudley Road, Manassas (703-361-1339; www.nps.gov/mana); $3; open dawn to dusk daily. Leashed Fidos are welcome to explore this historic Civil War site, and the Henry Hill cell phone tour makes it easy for their humans to listen to audio programs at nine stops on the Henry Hill Loop Trail (703-253-9002). The park also offers ranger-guided hikes over the several trails in the park, but note that pets are not allowed in the Henry Hill Visitor Center or Brawner Farm Interpretive Center.

From Northern Virginia, take I-66 west to Exit 47B (SR234 or Sudley Road) and from points south take I-95, Exit 152 (SR234). For more Civil War travel sites and special events, visit the National Park Service Sesquicentennial Commemoration website at www.nps.gov/features/waso/cw150th/index.html.

to Washington. Use the scenic parkway whenever possible, which runs parallel to the Potomac River, rather than I-95, I-395, or I-495, as these major commuter interstates are always backed up on weekdays.

While Alexandria does have both Metrorail and trolley service, Old Town is eminently walkable for you and your four-legged friend, and you'll find that many merchants put out complimentary water stations for visiting canines. You'll be spoiled for choice on accommodations, since Alexandria boasts not one but three of Kimpton's ultimate pet-friendly boutique hotels. Take your pooch on the Potomac Canine Cruise to see Mount Vernon from the river, followed by a visit to the pet-friendly estate grounds, where Fido can sniff out his Colonial ancestors. The Alexandria Farmers Market also welcomes canines, and the Kimpton's Hotel Monaco has weekly Yappy Hours for both local and visiting dogs.

Fredericksburg, about 50 miles south of Alexandria, is rich in Colonial and Civil War history, with a 40-block National Historic District that contains more than 350 original 18th- and 19th-century buildings. Among those are the house George Washington bought for his mother;

This local pooch takes a break from strolling around the Alexandria Farmers Market.

(Alexandria Convention & Visitors Association)

the house that his brother Charles built, which was later converted into the Rising Sun Tavern; and Kenmore, the plantation owned by George Washington's sister. Founded in 1728 and named for England's crown prince, Frederick Louis, the streets in the historic area are named for his family members: George, Caroline, Sophia, Princess Anne, William, and Amelia.

During the Civil War, the Fredericksburg area, one of the last lines of defense for Richmond, was the site of several bloody battles at Chancellorsville, Wilderness, Sunken Road, and the Spotsylvania Court House, with more than 100,000 dead and wounded soldiers. Many of those casualties from both sides are buried in local cemeteries, and Civil War buffs will want to visit the battlegrounds and museums.

Today, thanks to excellent rail service, Fredericksburg has become a commuter town for Northern Virginia and Washington workers who want to escape the major metropolitan area.

Less than an hour's drive from Richmond, Fredericksburg is an easy day trip or overnight stopping point on the way north on I-95 or US 1. Pick up a map at the visitor center and take Fido on a self-guided walk or leave your pal in the hotel to take the guided trolley tour. The town is filled with antiques shops, boutiques, and restaurants, and during the Christmas season, Virginia residents flock to Fredericksburg for the annual Candlelight Tour.

Nearby and Noteworthy in Northern Virginia

Both Alexandria and Fairfax are independent cities, although both are in Fairfax County, the most populous region of the state, covering 407 square miles. Named for Thomas Fairfax, the Sixth Lord Fairfax of Cameron, Fairfax was a land grant of five million acres from King Charles.

Today, Fairfax is an urban region known more for shopping than sightseeing, but if you're heading west toward the Shenandoah Valley or coming into Northern Virginia from that region, Tysons Corner (a shopping mecca in the Washington metropolitan area) boasts several pet-friendly luxury hotels.

SEE:

Arlington National Cemetery, 1 Memorial Drive, Fort Myer (703-271-7727; www.arlingtoncemetery.org); free; parking $1.75–2.50 per hour; open daily. Leashed pets are welcome to walk the beautiful grounds of Arlington National Cemetery and pay their respects at the gravesites of American heroes or observe the changing of the guard at the Tomb of the Unknowns. Created during the Civil War, the cemetery conducts an average of 27 funerals per day, so be respectful of the privacy of the families. You can pick up a map at the visitors center to find popular sites like the Kennedy graves or the Arlington House (Robert E. Lee Memorial) and there's also an information desk to help you locate a specific gravesite. The changing of the guard at the Tomb of the Unknowns runs every hour from Oct. 1 to March 31, and every half hour during the rest of the year. If you don't bring your four-legged friend, there's also an interpretive bus tour that leaves the visitor center continuously ($8.75 per person).

Great Falls National Park, 9200 Old Dominion Drive, McLean (703-285-2965; www.nps.gov/grfa/); $3. At this 800-acre park, the Potomac River flows over steep, jagged rocks into narrow Mather Gorge. There are three overlooks of the falls near the visitor center, as well as hiking trails and picnic areas. Leashed dogs are welcome on the trails, although some of the steeper cliff climbs may not be appropriate for Fido.

Smithsonian National Air & Space Museum Steven F. Udvar-Hazy Center, 14390 Air & Space Museum Pkwy, Chantilly (202-633-1000; http://airandspace.si.edu/udvarhazy/); free; public parking $15. Located close to Dulles International Airport, this museum is a companion to the one on the National Mall, offering an extended display of aviation and space artifacts and aircraft. You'll find the Lockheed SR-71 Blackbird, Boeing B-29 Superfortress *Enola Gay,* and Space Shuttle *Discovery*.

Wolftrap National Park for the Performing Arts, 1645 Trap Road, Vienna (703-255-1900; www.wolftrap.org); fees vary by show. One of the premier music venues in Virginia, Wolftrap offers unique concert experiences in the outdoor Filene Center, where you can bring a picnic or purchase food from onsite vendors and relax for an alfresco dinner under the stars on the spacious lawn seating area (reserved seating also available). During the winter months, intimate performances in the Barns of Wolftrap allow music lovers a close-up view.

STAY:

Ritz-Carlton Tysons Corner, 1700 Tysons Boulevard, McLean (703-506-4300; www.ritzcarlton.com/tysons); from $239 per night. The luxurious Ritz-Carlton is attached to the Tysons Galleria shopping complex, so you don't even have to go out the front door of the hotel to indulge in some retail therapy. Relax in the day spa after your shopping spree, or just kick back with your four-legged friend and enjoy your elegant accommodations. Pets up to 30 pounds are welcome with a $250 fee per pet per stay, and canine guests receive dog treats and toys, as well as loaner bowls and a "Woof" door sign. At Christmas, the lobby of the hotel turns into a gingerbread wonderland with special thematic displays made by the hotel's pastry team.

Sheraton Premiere at Tysons Corner, 8661 Leesburg Pike, Vienna (703-448-1234; www.sheratontysonscorner.com); from $220 per night. A mere 10 minutes from Dulles International Airport, the Sheraton features a state-of-the-art fitness center and a 24th-floor lounge with panoramic views of the region. Located just a mile from Wolftrap, this is a good choice if you're seeing a show. Pets up to 80 pounds are welcome with no additional fees, and you can request a dog bed and loaner bowls when you reserve your room.

Westin Tysons Corner, 7801 Leesburg Pike, Falls Church (703-893-1340; www.westintysonscornerhotel.com/); from $260 per night. The 405-room Westin is an oasis of modern tranquility, featuring Westin's trademark Heavenly Beds, even for Fido! Request Fido's in advance when you book and it will be waiting in your room, along with other amenities including loaner bowls and cleanup bags. Dogs up to 40 pounds are welcome with no additional fees.

Visit Fairfax County www.fxva.com

East of Fredericksburg, across the Rappahannock River, is the Northern Neck, the birthplace of George Washington and a favorite vacation spot for Virginians. The 90-mile peninsula is surrounded on three sides by the waters of the Rappahannock and Potomac Rivers and the Chesapeake Bay, and the quaint seaside town of Irvington is one of the state's most popular resort areas. Ironically, Ferry Farm, Washington's boyhood home, was perilously close

to becoming the site of a discount store, but historians and preservationists banded together to make the farm a national landmark. Ongoing archaeological digs are still uncovering parts of the original home, and thousands of artifacts from Washington's formative years. Two other US presidents, James Monroe and James Madison, were also born here, but unfortunately their family homes have not survived; simple markers designate the sites of their former estates. Other historic attractions in the area include Christ Church, built by Robert "King" Carter, and Stratford Hall, the birthplace of Robert E. Lee. Irvington hosts a weekly farmers market for

Fredericksburg's Holiday Candlelight Tour draws visitors from around the state.

(Courtesy of Fredericksburg Area Tourism)

"Yes, Mom . . . get me some bison!" says this Irvington pooch at the farmers market.

you and Fido to browse (don't be surprised to see the local chefs shopping for your dinner!), and there are several pet-friendly wineries in the area for a taste of local produce in a glass.

From Fredericksburg, getting to the Northern Neck is easy, as both SR 3 and US 17 south connect to US 360, which crosses the Rappahannock River at the Tappahannock Bridge. About 55 miles from Richmond and 75 miles from Washington, the Northern Neck is a prime summer destination for Virginians.

Irvington's main street is lined with lovely Victorian homes.

Whether you want to soak up some history and scour boutiques for treasures of old or soak up the sun and sail the rivers and the Chesapeake Bay, both Fredericksburg and the Northern Neck are full of fun for you and your furry friend.

Northern Neck Trails and Tales

Captain John Smith first visited the Northern Neck in 1608, and today you can follow in his wake on America's first national water trail, the Captain John Smith Chesapeake National Historic Trail (www.smithtrail .net). Explore the same waterways Smith saw four hundred years ago by kayak or sailboat.

Birders will want to trek the Northern Neck loop of the Virginia Birding and Wildlife Trail (www.dgif.virginia.gov/vbwt), to check out the spectacular scenery and wide array of wildlife and bird species along the waterfront and in the forested areas that George Washington explored as a boy.

If cycling is more your style, try the eight loop trails of the Northern Neck section of the Potomac Heritage National Scenic Trail network (www.potomacheritage.net/category/virginias-northern-neck).

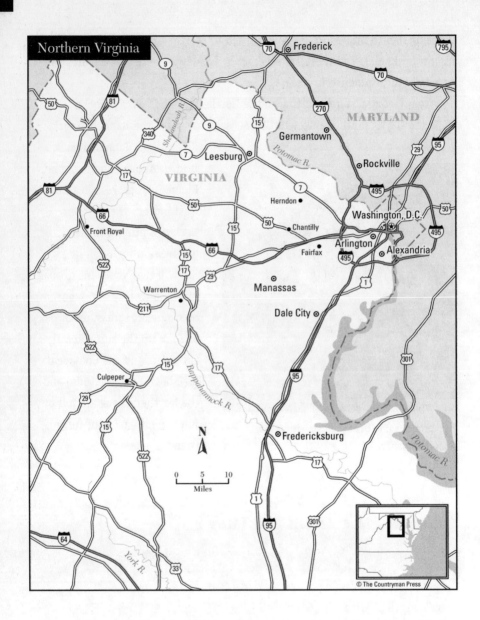

Northern Virginia

© The Countryman Press

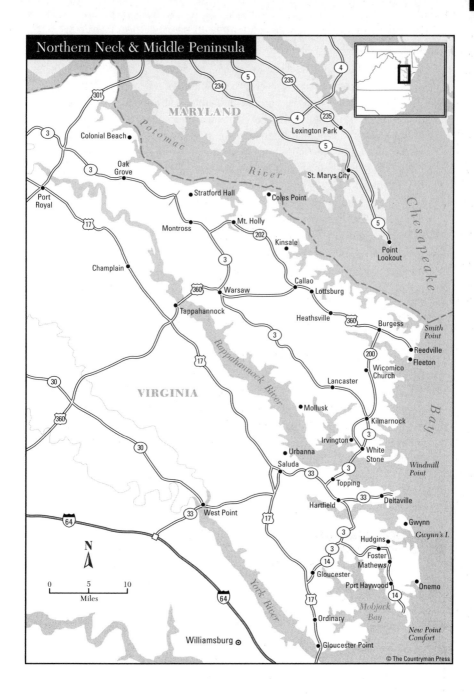

Northern Neck & Middle Peninsula

My Favorite Neck of the Woods

Since I grew up in this area, here are a few of my hometown favorites.

—GW

Gunston Hall, 10709 Gunston Road, SR 242 off US 1, Lorton (703-550-9220; www.gunstonhall.org); $10; 9:30–5:30 daily. George Mason IV was the principal author of the Virginia Declaration of Rights, one of the first of Virginia's statesmen to call for fundamental liberties such as freedom of the press and religious tolerance. His home, Gunston Hall, was the center of a 5,500-acre corn and tobacco plantation on the Potomac River, just a few miles south of Mount Vernon, and is considered to be one of the finest examples of Georgian architecture from the Colonial period, with elaborate carved woodwork. The original gardens, with gravel paths and 250-year-old boxwood allée surround the home.

Mason Neck State Park, Gunston Road, SR 242 off US 1 (703-339-2385; www.dcr.virginia.gov/state_parks/mas.shtml); from $4. Located on a peninsula bounded by Pohick Bay, Belmont Bay, and the Potomac River, Mason Neck State Park is home to bald eagles and one of the largest heronries on the East Coast. There are several miles of hiking and biking trails, but no swimming areas or overnight accommodations. This is a great natural park for long walks with your pal.

Workhouse Arts Center, 9601 Ox Road, Lorton (703-584-2900; www.lortonarts.org); free; fees for classes, and performances vary. If you lived in Lorton before the 21st century, that address always prompted people to say, "Oh, you live near the prison?" The prison, built for overspill from the DC Department of Corrections, was closed in 2001 and repurposed as an art and education complex, featuring galleries, performing arts, and a variety of classes.

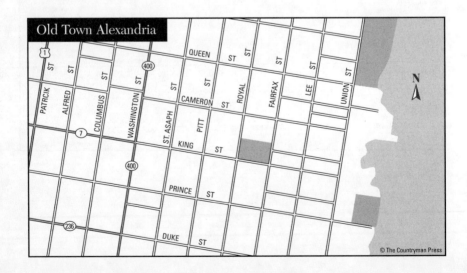

Best Beds: Comfy Sleeps for You and Your Canine Family

General's Ridge Vineyard & Winery, 1618 Weldon Drive, Hague (703-313-9742 or 804-493-0226; www.generalsridgevineyard.com); from $179 per night. Set on over 100 tranquil acres, General's Ridge offers elegant accommodations in the 150-year-old Manor House and Vineyard Views Cottage, and well-behaved dogs are welcomed by the owners' two friendly black Labs. There's plenty of room to roam and run on the plantation, and you can even take your pal to the tasting room while you sample the vineyard's bounty. An additional fee of $25 per night for Fido applies.

Hope & Glory Inn, 65 Tavern Road, Irvington (804-438-6053; www .hopeandglory.com); from $205 per night. Settle into a cozy cottage with your furry family at the Hope & Glory Inn, consistently ranked among the top 10 inns in the country. The former 1890 schoolhouse has six charming rooms (think vintage shabby-chic) and there are six quaint garden cottages for more space and privacy. Pets are welcome to enjoy your Chesapeake Bay sojourn for an additional $40 fee, although they must remain leashed in public areas. Be sure to make a reservation for the popular Dining Hall, and you may want to leave

your pal for a nap while you enjoy the cocktail cruise on the inn's 42-foot oyster boat.

Hotel Monaco, 480 King Street, Alexandria (703-549-6080; www .monaco-alexandria.com); from $339 per night. Located in the heart of Old Town Alexandria, the Kimpton's Hotel Monaco is the premier pet-friendly destination, with stylish accommodations for you and your furry family, as well as top-shelf amenities and activities for Fido. Their Director of Pet Relations is a Bichon Frise named Charlie, who not only greets four-legged guests but also makes sure a complimentary toy, along with a comfy loaner bed and bowls, are delivered

Snacks are served at Yappy Hour at the Hotel Monaco. (Courtesy of Hotel Monaco)

The Hotel Monaco in Alexandria, a Kimpton property, hosts a weekly Yappy Hour.

(Courtesy of Hotel Monaco/David Phelps)

to Fido's room at check-in. From April through October, on Tuesday and Thursday evenings at 5 P.M., the hotel hosts a Yappy Hour (doggy hors d'oeurves included!) where local residents can mingle with guests from around the world. You can also dine with your pooch at Jackson's at any time. As with all of Kimpton's boutique hotels, there is never any weight or size restriction or additional fee for canine guests.

Lorien Hotel & Spa, 1600 King Street, Alexandria (703-894-3434; www.lorienhotelandspa.com); from $220 per night. Located just a few blocks from the George Washington Masonic Memorial, the Lorien exudes serenity, with luxurious modern style in an Old World setting. With all the amenities of home, from plush spa robes to loaner bicycles, the Lorien also makes sure four-legged guests have every-

The Lorien Hotel & Spa in Old Town combines modern aesthetics with Old World charm.

(Courtesy of the Lorien Hotel&Spa/David Phelps)

thing they need, from dog leashes, comfy beds, and bowls to a "Very Important Pet" amenity delivered at check-in. While you're getting a relaxing massage at the spa, the concierge will be happy to arrange one for your pal too!

Morrison House, 116 South Alfred Street, Alexandria (703-838-8000; www.morrisonhouse.com); from $259 per night. Experience luxury Colonial-style at Morrison House, the longest-standing AAA four-diamond property in Virginia. With only 45 rooms and suites, this hotel has the intimacy of a B&B combined with the modern amenities

and stellar service you expect from a grand hotel. Also located in the heart of Old Town, the Morrison House offers an "Incredible Journey Pet Package" that includes deluxe accommodations, in-room beds, bowls, and pet food, and a "Classic Tail" of your choice: one of four great dog books.

Richard Johnston Inn, 711 Caroline Street, Fredericksburg (540-899-7606; www.therichard johnstoninn.com); from $175 per night. Constructed in 1770 and named for the Fredericksburg mayor who called it home in the 1800s, the Richard Johnston Inn

The Morrison House, with 45 guest rooms and suites, combines the intimacy of a B&B with top-shelf amenities and service for you and your four-legged friend.

(Courtesy of Morrison House/David Phelps)

has a big "Pets Welcome" banner on their homepage. Four-legged guests are welcome in two of the rooms (Isabella Suite and Kitchen House) that are directly off the courtyard for an additional $25 fee (must be paid in cash), and the inn asks that you don't allow your pal on the furniture or to be left in the room alone. The room rate includes a continental breakfast on weekdays and full breakfast on weekends, and the inn also offers free Wi-Fi. Located in the heart of the historic district, the inn books up early and a one-night deposit is required with your reservation.

The Tides Inn, 480 King Carter Drive, Irvington (804-438-5000; www.tidesinn.com); from $225 per night. A member of the Leading

Hotels of the World, the Tides Inn has been a favorite escape for Virginians for the past 50 years. The tranquil resort has a full-service spa, a championship golf course surrounding a 50-acre lake, a private marina, and some of the friendliest staff in the state. Homey touches like complimentary lemonade and cookies on the portico, loaner bicycles, a croquet lawn, and s'mores around the fire pit will make you feel like a guest at a friend's home. Take a sailing lesson, charter a fishing excursion, or bike into the quaint town of Irvington to peruse the boutiques and farmers market. The resort's Pampered Paws Program welcomes members of your furry family up to 75 pounds with a onetime $35 fee, and in-

Gather around the Tides Inn firepit in the evening for s'mores.

Guests gather in the cozy lounge at the Tides Inn for coffee in the morning or sing-a-alongs in the evening.

cludes amenities like a comfy bed, barrel of doggy treats, water bowl, and waste bags. You'll also get a map of strategically located pet relief areas on the resort property, and the concierge will be happy to arrange pet sitting, grooming, or dog walking as needed.

Camping and Cabins

Westmoreland State Park, SR 3, Washington (804-493-8821; www .dcr.virginia.gov/state_parks/wes .shtml); camping from $20; cabins from $59. Snuggle up in a cozy cabin in Westmoreland State Park, a 1,311-acre expanse that is a neighbor to the boyhood homes of George Washington and Robert E. Lee. The park runs along the Potomac River, with spectacular views from Horsehead Cliffs.

Leashed pets are allowed on trails, but not in swimming or concession areas, and pets can stay in both the campground and cabins for an additional nightly fee of $5 for camping and $10 for cabins. All cabins are fully furnished with linens and dishes, and most have fireplaces.

The Northern Neck offers tranquil river views.

Famous Four-Legged Virginians

HOUNDS & HISTORY AT THE FREDERICKSBURG DOG FAIR

Every fall, Fredericksburg celebrates its four-legged residents with a parade and a day of dog-centric events and entertainment in the heart of the city. The event dates back to 1698, when English settlers began trading with the local Native Americans, who coveted the hunting dogs bred by the newcomers. What was then called "the Dog Mart" grew into an event that drew thousands of professional hunting packs and spectators, becoming more of a dog show than a dog sale. Members of the Patawomeck, Mattaponi, and Pamunkey tribes participated in the event throughout much of the 20th century, and *National Geographic* magazine profiled the historic canine gathering in the 1950s.

Today, the Fredericksburg Dog Fair includes a Masquerade Parade that winds through downtown Fredericksburg to Riverside Park, where the King & Queen canines are crowned. The all-day festival includes live entertainment and a variety of pet events and pet vendors, with proceeds distributed to local animal-welfare groups.

www.fredericksburgdogfair.com

Best Bowls: Restaurants Worth a Sitter

Gadsby's Tavern, 34 North Royal Street, Alexandria (703-746-4242; www.gadsbystavernrestaurant.com). If you happened to visit this tavern in the 1770s, you might have been seated next to George Washington, Thomas Jefferson, or the Lee brothers. As it is, the history of the tavern alone is worth a visit, but while the décor is Colonial, the food is inspired by, but not stuck in, the 18th century. You'll find some Old Dominion favorites like peanut soup, along with French classics (Jefferson's favorite) like beef bordelaise. If you want to eat like the father of our country, the menu lists George Washington's favorite as grilled duck breast with scalloped potatoes and corn pudding.

Goolrick's Pharmacy, 901 Caroline Street, Fredericksburg (540-373-3411; www.goolricks.com). Goolrick's Pharmacy opened in 1869, and the soda fountain, which debuted in 1912, is one of the oldest continuously operating in the United States. Try a malt or an egg cream for a blast of the past, or grab a light lunch here while you're exploring the historic district.

The oldest continuously operating soda fountain in America, Goolrick's still serves up great food in downtown Fredericksburg.

(Courtesy of Fredericksburg Area Tourism)

Nate's Trick Dog Café, 4357 Irvington Road, Irvington (804-438-6363; www.trickdogcafe.com). One of the most popular restaurants on the Northern Neck, with a hip urban vibe, Nate's has created its own urban legend surrounding the canine statue in its foyer. The story goes that the owner found the statue in the basement of the Opera House after the 1917 Great Fire that burned most of Irvington. He took it home and told his family that it was a "trick dog" because you didn't have to feed or water it and it would always "sit and stay." Today, petting the trick dog is said to bring good luck. The restaurant serves everything from filet mignon to duck breast, on plates inscribed with "sit-stay."

Restaurant Eve, 110 South Pitt Street, Alexandria (703-706-0450; www.restauranteve.com). If it's good enough for the President and First Lady's anniversary dinner, it should probably be on your list. Chef Cathal Armstrong is a local and national foodie favorite for his innovative food and restaurant concepts (he and his wife, Meshelle, have six different eateries in the area). Originally from Dublin, Chef Armstrong offers two distinct dining experiences under one roof and promises guests a "gastronomic epiphany": worth a splurge is the 34-seat Chef's Tasting Room, which is a showcase of culinary chops, from heirloom-tomato tarts to butter-poached Maine lobster with

Nate's Trick Dog appeals to dog lovers and foodies alike.

Eastern Shore corn. No less appetizing, but much less formal (and about half the price) is the Bistro and Lounge, where the chef's passion for sustainable meat and seafood may show up as crabcakes and fried oysters or good old country ham.

Vermilion, 1120 King Street, Alexandria (703-684-9669; www .vermilionrestaurant.com). President and Mrs. Obama have celebrated Valentine's Day at Vermilion, known for its farm-to-table regional American cuisine, and while the White House garden isn't on the restaurant's list of

Take your pal on a stroll through Old Town Fredericksburg and do some window shopping at the many antiques stores and boutiques.

(Courtesy of Fredericksburg Area Tourism)

purveyors, most of its food comes from Virginia, Maryland, and Pennsylvania. Chef Tony Chittum's style has been called "deceptively simple American fare" infused with his passion for Italian and Greek food. Try to catch one of his weekly Farm Table Dinners to taste the best sustainable products of the region. Since menus change often according to what's in season, it's impossible to list specific items, but you can expect to see local favorites like Maryland blue crab and Eastern Shore oysters, as well as the best local produce and meat.

Tail Waggers: Fido's Favorite Outings

Alexandria Farmers Market, 301 King Street, Market Square, Alexandria (703-746-3200; http:// alexandriava.gov/FarmersMarket); free; Saturdays 7 A.M. to noon; free parking in Market garage. Local farmers and artists have been selling their wares in this plaza since 1753: even George Washington sent his produce from Mount Vernon to the market here. Well-behaved leashed pets are welcome to browse the stalls along with their humans.

Athena Vineyards, 3138 Jessie Ball DuPont Highway (804-580-4944; www.athenavineyards.com); open Wednesday to Sunday. The owner's Yorkie may be waiting for your arrival in this Northern Neck tasting room and gift shop, which,

Ain't Nothin' but a Hound Dog

Virginia is one of only a handful of states to have an official state dog, and the Old Dominion's canine mascot, the American Foxhound, dates back to the days of George Washington. Everyone knows Washington is the father of our country, but Virginia foxhunters also know him as the father of our state dog. Washington was an avid foxhunter and dog breeder who combined English Foxhounds with several larger French staghounds he received from the Marquis de Lafayette to create the canine lineage that continues today. However, if you're talking to one of the state's passionate foxhunting aficionados, never call a foxhound a dog; it is always referred to as a hound.

due to its compact size, may not be a great place for large dogs (big wagging tails + delicate displays = trouble). Athena wines make great gifts, as this winery is known for its unique bottles: Galleon Treasure Red in a bottle shaped like a ship, Sweet Notes Red in a guitar-shaped bottle, and special holiday decanters.

General's Ridge Vineyard & Winery, 1618 Weldon Drive, Hague (703-313-9742 or 804-493-0226; www.generalsridgevineyard.com); open Thursday to Sunday. The two resident Labs at the vineyard will give you and your pooch a wagging welcome at this beautiful Northern Neck estate, set on 100 acres. Fido is even welcome in the tasting room.

Ingleside Plantation Vineyards, 5872 Leedstown Road, Oak Grove (804-224-8687; www.inglesidevineyards.com). One of Virginia's oldest wineries, Ingleside, on the Northern Neck, has won the Virginia Governor's Cup several times, as well as national and international awards. Taste several of the 18 varieties made from estate-grown grapes, from Viognier and Sauvignon Blanc to Sangiovese and Cabernet Franc. Four-legged visitors are welcome on the grounds and in the tasting room.

Irvington Farmers Market, Irvington Town Commons, Irvington (www.irvingtonva.org); first Saturday of the month from May through November. Don't be surprised the see all the local chefs shopping at the Irvington Farmers Market for locally grown produce, from heirloom tomatoes to canteloupes. Part market and part craft fair; you and your pooch can meet local two- and four-legged residents as you browse the arts and crafts stalls. Pick up some lunch and relax at one of the shady picnic tables on the Commons.

Mount Vernon, 3200 Mount Vernon Memorial Highway (703-780-2000; www.mountvernon.org); $15; free parking; open daily, 365 days a year. You'll probably want to visit Mount Vernon twice: once with your BFF (best furry friend) so the two of you can explore the gardens and grounds of George and Martha Washington's estate, and once without your pal to tour the mansion and museum exhibits. Perched on the banks of the Potomac River, the 500 acres (out of the original 8,000-acre tract) contain numerous outbuildings, as well as the tomb where the Washingtons are buried.

Potomac River Canine Cruise, Virginia Dock, Alexandria (703-684-0580; www.potomacriverboatco .com); $15 humans; free for Fido. Take a 40-minute riverboat cruise around the Alexandria seaport with your furry friend for a relaxing and scenic tour of the Colonial area.

Yappy Hour at Hotel Monaco, 480 King Street, Alexandria (703-549-6080; www.monaco-alexandria .com). Introduce your four-legged friend to locals and hotel guests from around the world at the Hotel Monaco's weekly Yappy Hours. Held from April through October on Tuesday and Thursday evenings at

Fidos line up for tickets to the Potomac Riverboat Company's Canine Cruise.

(Alexandria Convention & Visitors Association)

Leader of the Pack

The earliest records of Virginia foxhunting come from George Washington's diaries and the letters of Thomas, Sixth Lord Fairfax, who is credited with instituting the first organized group foxhunt in the state, a territory still hunted today by the Blue Ridge Hunt. Fairfax County is named for the passionate foxhunter. Legend has it that when Congress was in session and the hounds were running, congressmen would run out of the Capitol, hop on their horses, and join the chase. Today, foxhunting is still a popular sport in Virginia, but note that Old Dominion foxhunters do *not* kill the fox. In fact, the 19 hunt clubs in the state registered with the Masters of Foxhounds Association take care of the foxes in their respective territories, feeding them during the cold winter months and adding medications to their food to keep them healthy.

5 P.M., Yappy Hours have become a community tradition for pet-loving Alexandria residents and visitors alike. Complimentary pet treats and water bowls keep Fidos happy, while human guests enjoy the fare of Jackson 20's bar menu. Dogs must be leashed and wearing a current rabies tag.

◎ Sweet Treats and Canine Chic: Where to Shop with Your BFF

Barkley Square Pets, 311 North Washington Street, Alexandria (703-329-1043; www.barkleysquare .com). From peanut butter cookies to Dog Beer, you can find every kind of treat imaginable here. You can even order a canine Thanksgiving feast or doggy sushi, and there's a small café area where you can sit with your pal while he chows down.

Dog Krazy, 1011 Caroline Street, Fredericksburg (540-373-4168; www.dogkrazyva.com). Take Fido to the "barkery" counter at Dog Krazy for a gourmet cupcake or treat, while you shop for cool accessories and gifts.

Nature's Nibbles, 2601 Mount Vernon Avenue, Alexandria (703-931-5241; www.naturesnibbles .com). Specializing in all-natural pet foods, treats, supplements, and grooming supplies, Nature's Nibbles carries top-of-the-line brands.

Pet Sage, 2391 South Dove Street, Alexandria (703-299-5044; www.pet sage.com). Pet Sage is a New Age pet health store, with everything from foods to books on behavior and beyond. If holistic works for your pooch, this is the place to find all kinds of therapeutic products and natural foods.

The Old Town Farmers Market draws lots of four-legged visitors.

(Alexandria Convention & Visitors Association)

◉ Big-Box Stores

Petco www.petco.com. In Alexandria: 6612 Richmond Highway, (703-660-1300). In Fredericksburg: 5717 Plank Road (540-785-0137).

PetSmart www.petsmart.com. In Alexandria: 3351 Jefferson Davis Highway (703-739-4844). In Fredericksburg: 9751 Jefferson Davis Highway (540-834-4336); 1421 Carl D Silver Parkway (540-785-9851); 27 South Gateway Drive (540-372-1258).

♛ A Day of Beauty: Best Pooch Primping

ALEXANDRIA

For Pet's Sake, 1537 North Quaker Lane, Alexandria (703-931-2600; www.forpetssakeofalexandria.com).

This pet salon has three decades of accolades and awards for caring service and excellent grooming of all sizes and breeds.

Hairy Situations Dog Grooming, 1552 Potomac Greens Drive, Alexandria (703-518-3030; www.hairysituationsgrooming.com).

The name is humorous, but these groomers are serious about providing gentle and stress-free grooming in a human-style salon environment. Due to their policy of "wide" appointment slots that guarantee they won't have to rush their canine clients, you may have to book in advance.

Old Towne School for Dogs, 529 Oronoco Street, Alexandria (703-836-7643; http://otsfd.com). Book early for the popular grooming salon here, one of the most popular in the city. The salon uses the Prima bathing system and blow-drys clients by hand. This is a one-stop pet palace with a retail shop and professional training classes, in addition to the salon, all under one roof.

Wash That Dog, 105 Moncure Drive, Alexandria (703-299-9274; www.oldtowndoggiewash.com). Formerly the Old Town Doggie Wash, this BYOD (bring your own dog) self-service shop has everything you need to clean up your canine.

FREDERICKSBURG

A Handsome Hound Grooming Salon, 103 1/2 William Street, Fredericksburg (540-368-9663; http://petgroomingfredericksburg.com). Despite the name, this salon isn't just for male Fidos; feminine doggy divas get the full treatment as well!

Paw Prints Salon, 10821 Courthouse Road, Fredericksburg (540-710-5689; www.pawprintssalon.com). Paw Prints has a hydro bathing system and promises a true "spa" experience. Groomers here have extensive show-dog experience.

Tails of Idlewild, 2011 Idlewild Boulevard, Fredericksburg (540-370-0130; www.tailsofidlewild.com). These experienced groomers are a great choice for large dogs

and arthritic seniors: they have a state-of-the-art, Ultra-lift tub that lowers to 8 inches to provide a safe and comfortable entrance.

♥ Play Dates: Doggy Daycare

Dog's Best Friend, 2000-A Jefferson Davis Highway (US 1), Alexandria (www.yourdogsbestfriends.com); call for rate quote. Dog's Best Friend has a 4,600-square-foot facility (indoor only) for cage-free boarding and daycare that they call "state of the arf," with special vulcanized rubber flooring to protect your pal's paws and joints during a day of play. They also offer pet-sitting and dog-walking services, which may be better for visitors, since they have an admissions and orientation process. The facility insists on an orientation visit and interview before accepting boarders; visitors who will only be in the area for a short time may want to check on the pet-sitting and dog-walking services instead.

Dogtopia of Alexandria, 3121 Colvin Street, Alexandria (703-751-7387; www.dogdaycare.com/alexandria); boarding from $20; daycare $35 single day; $32 for five-day pass. With open playcare and webcam monitoring, you can check in on your pooch while you're away. Check out the Spa Package, which includes playtime and a full bath and groom.

Four Paws Resort, 29 Baron Park Road, Fredericksburg (540-310-4814; www.4pawsresort.com); boarding from $27; luxury suites from $42; daycare from $16. With totally cage-free boarding and daycare, and huge indoor and outdoor play areas, Four Paws promises up to 10 hours of playtime and personal attention a day.

Worth a Sitter: Sights to See without Fido

TRAVEL TIP: Purchase a Timeless Ticket ($32) at the Fredericksburg Visitor Center, good for admission to nine attractions, including George Washington's boyhood home, and save more than 40 percent over individual admissions (www.visitfred.com).

Fredericksburg/Spotsylvania National Military Park, 1013 Lafayette Boulevard at Sunken Road (540-373-6122; ww.nps.gov frsp); free. The mammoth 9,000-acre park encompasses four battlefields and four historic buildings. See Chancellorsville, where General Stonewall Jackson was mistakenly wounded by his own troops, Sunken Road, where the Confederate forces pushed back Union forces, and the Spotsylvania Court House battlefields. During the tourist season, park rangers lead guided walking tours. Chatham Manor, the former home of William Fitzhugh (a contemporary of George Washington and Thomas Jefferson) is also in the park area. The home was commandeered by Union forces during the war.

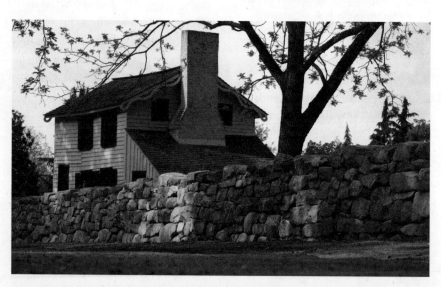

Park rangers lead guided tours of Sunken Road, where Robert E. Lee successfully blocked Union forces from marching on Richmond. (Courtesy of Fredericksburg Area Tourism)

George Washington Birthplace National Monument, 1732 Pope's Creek Road, Oak Grove (804-224-1732; www.nps.gov/gewa); free. Since this is a National Park Service site, Fido is allowed on the grounds but not in the historic area, which includes the living Colonial area and visitor center, with artifacts found during the archaeological digs, so it's best to leave the pooch with a sitter for this one.

George Washington's Ferry Farm, 268 Kings Highway, Fredericksburg (540-370-0732; www.kenmore.org); $8 or combo with Kenmore $15; also included in Fredericksburg Timeless Ticket. Washington lived here, just across the Rappahannock River from Fredericksburg, from the age of six until he was 19. Once called the Home Farm, it was re-named Ferry Farm because the ferry to Fredericksburg docked there. Ongoing archaeological digs have uncovered the original location of the house, as well as many artifacts from Washington's time. Take a self-guided tour of the 80-acre riverside estate and gardens.

George Washington Masonic Memorial, 101 Callahan Drive, Alexandria (703-683-2007; http://gwmemorial.org); $8 guided tour including tower; $5 self-guided lower floors; free parking. George Washington joined the Masonic Lodge in Fredericksburg in 1752 and took his inaugural oath of office using a Bible from a New York Masonic Lodge. He was a charter master of Alexandria Lodge No.22, renamed the Alexandria-Washington Lodge after his death. The original lodge was destroyed by a fire in 1871, and in the early 20th century, Masons throughout America designed a plan for a new lodge that would also be a memorial to the man they considered to be the living emblem of the Freemason creed: to improve themselves and their communities. The Memorial contains hundreds of

The George Washington Masonic National Memorial in Alexandria is still a meeting place for Freemasons, as well as a tourist attraction.

(Alexandria Convention & Visitors Association)

Washington artifacts and is still an active meeting place for both local and visiting Masons, as well as a performance center and research facility.

Historic Christ Church, 420 Christ Church Road, Irvington (804-438-6855; www.christchurch1735.org); $5 donation requested. George Washington was three years old when Christ Church was completed in 1735. Built by one of Virginia's most prominent citizens, Robert "King" Carter, the church looks much the same today as it did in Washington's time and, with its rare triple-decker pulpit, is said to be one of the finest examples of a Colonial-era church.

Mount Vernon, 3200 Mount Vernon Memorial Highway (703-780-2000; www.mountvernon.org); $15; free parking; open daily 365 days a year. The most famous of George Washington's homes, Mount Vernon sits on the banks of the Potomac River, just 7 miles south of Alexandria. Privately owned by the Mount Vernon Ladies Association, a nonprofit organization formed in 1853 to preserve the estate, the 500-acre property has been open to the public since 1860. Start at the Ford Orientation Center for an overview, visit the Donald W. Reynolds Museum and Education Center, where you can watch films about Washington's life and see

Historic Christ Church was built by Virginia's Carter family.

more than 700 personal artifacts, tour the mansion and outbuildings, and stroll through the beautiful grounds. Pets are welcome on the grounds, so you may want to return with your furry friend to walk through history.

Stratford Hall, 483 Great House Road, Stratford (804-493-8038; www.stratfordhall.org); $10. Four generations of the Lee family called Stratford Hall home, including Richard Henry Lee and Francis Lightfoot Lee, both signers of the Declaration of Independence, Revolutionary war hero "Light Horse Harry" Lee, and his son, Civil War general Robert E. Lee. Set on the Potomac River on 1,900 acres, the Colonial estate built in the 1730s has beautiful gardens and an extensive collection of period pieces in the Great House.

The Washington Family Homes in Fredericksburg: Kenmore, Mary Washington House, Rising Sun Tavern (included in Fredericksburg Timeless Ticket). George Washington grew up on Ferry Farm just across the river from Fredericksburg, but in later years, his sister, brother, and mother had homes in the city. **Kenmore** (1201 Washington Avenue; www.kenmore.org) was built by Washington's brother-in-law, Colonel Fielding Lewis, as the centerpiece of a 1,300-acre plantation. Lewis lost his fortune supply-ing Washington's troops during the Revolutionary War, and his widow was forced to sell the home after his death. In 1772, Washington purchased a home for his mother and doubled its size while renovating it for her. The **Mary Washington House** (1200 Charles Street; www.apva.org/marywashingtonhouse) retains the original boxwoods in the gorgeous gardens where she loved spending her time. Washington's brother, Charles, built a home in Fredericksburg as well, which in later years became the Rising Sun Tavern (1304 Caroline Street; www.apva.org/risingsuntavern), a favorite watering hole for patriots like the Lee brothers, Washington himself, Patrick Henry, and Thomas Jefferson.

To get an overview of the history of Fredericksburg, take the trolley tour that leaves from the Visitor Center in Old Town. (Courtesy of Fredericksburg Area Tourism)

Shenandoah National Park: Virginia's Premier Mountain Getaway

All across the Nation . . . people are starting out for their vacations in national and state parks. Those people will put up at roadside camps or pitch their tents under the stars, with an open fire to cook by, with the smell of the woods, and the wind in the trees. They will forget the rush and the strain of all the other long weeks of the year, and for a short time at least, the days will be good for their bodies and good for their souls. Once more they will lay hold of the perspective that comes to men and women who every morning and every night can lift up their eyes to Mother Nature.

—Franklin D. Roosevelt,
Address at the Dedication of Shenandoah National Park

On July 3, 1936, President Franklin D. Roosevelt spoke at the dedication ceremony for Shenandoah National Park, and his words still resonate today. Shenandoah National Park continues to be one of the most popular national parks in America, providing recreation and respite that soothes the human spirit, while preserving the natural beauty of Virginia's Blue Ridge Mountains and wildlife for generations to come. Built by the Civilian Conservation Corps (CCC), the park and others like it throughout the country provided desperately needed jobs during the Great Depression. A bronze statue of a CCC worker at the Byrd Visitor Center, one of 32 across the

(Continued on page 169)

One of the many scenic overlooks throughout the park and on Skyline Drive.

Fido 411

Here are some of the most important numbers to have when you arrive in Shenandoah National Park:

✚ 24-hour Emergency Veterinarians

Blue Ridge Veterinary Associates, 120 East Cornwell Lane, Purcellville (540-338-7387; www.blueridgevets.com). This animal clinic also offers 24-hour emergency services and is about 51 miles from the park and Luray, VA.

Greenbrier Emergency Animal Hospital, 370 Greenbriar Drive, Charlottesville (434-202-1616; www.greenbrier-emergency.com). About 45 miles from the park in Charlottesville, Greenbrier is open 24/7, 365 days a year, including major holidays.

Shenandoah Valley Regional Veterinary Emergency Services, 465 Lee Highway (in the Verona Shopping Center), Verona (540-248-1051; www.svres.com). Monday to Thursday 6 P.M. to 8 A.M. and Friday 6 P.M. to Monday 8 A.M.

Valley Veterinary Emergency and Referral Center (VVREC), 210 Costello Drive, Winchester (540-662-7811; http://vverc.com). VVREC is the only critical-care animal hospital in the valley, with an onsite surgery, laboratory, and radiation department. More than 50 regional veterinarians refer patients to VVREC for emergency care and the clinic accepts Care Credit, as well as most major credit cards. If you're in Shenandoah National Park, this clinic is the closest with 24-hour service, about 36 miles away.

Animal Poison Control Center—ASPCA (888-426-4435 or www.aspca.org/pet-care/poison-control/). If you think your pet may have ingested a poisonous substance or animal, help is available 24 hours a day, 365 days a year.

To find an emergency-care veterinarian from your smartphone, check the following websites for the closest location.

www.vetsnearyou.com, www.localvets.com, or **www.animalclinics nearyou.com** Enter the zip code of your location and it will bring up a list and map of the closest veterinarians.

To find a 24-hour pharmacy, check the store-locator search on one of these websites:

CVS: www.cvs.com

Walgreens: www.walgreens.com

RX List: www.rxlist.com/pharmacy/local_locations_pharmacies.htm

D-Tails

Shenandoah National Park Emergency Services (800) 732-0911

Shenandoah National Park www.nps.gov/shen/index.htm

Park Pet Regulations www.nps.gov/shen/planyourvisit/pets.htm

Park Pet-Friendly Accommodations/Aramark www.visitshenandoah.com

Oh, Ranger www.ohranger.com This comprehensive website has a wealth of valuable information on all national parks, with a free iPhone app you can take along on the trails.

nation, honors the work of the corps.

The largest treeless area in the park, Big Meadows, was the site of one of the first CCC camps and of the park's dedication ceremony. Once covering more than 1,000 acres filled with wildflowers and blueberries, today the National Park Service (NPS) must control the wood shrubs and trees that have encroached on the open meadow for the animals who feed on the more than 270 species of plants in the flat, grassy area.

Located about 75 miles west of Washington, DC, the 200,000-acre park stretches for 105 miles from the northern entrance at Front Royal to the southernmost entrance at Rockfish Gap (also the northern entrance to the Blue Ridge Parkway). Called Skyline Drive, the point-to-point route is one of the most popular scenic drives in America, especially in the fall, when the mountains are ablaze with color. Part of one of the oldest mountain ranges in the world, the Appalachians, Shenandoah is filled with unique rock formations and waterfalls, more than 500 miles of trails, 100 species of trees, 330 species of animals, and 1,100 flowering plants. Bears and bobcats share the forest with chipmunks and squirrels, raccoons and rabbits, white-tailed deer and groundhogs.

The National Park Service oversees Shenandoah National Park.

Travel 411

The nearest emergency veterinary services are about an hour's drive from Shenandoah National Park. If you're in the north end of the park, Winchester may be your closest option, but if you're farther south, Charlottesville or Verona, near Staunton, may be the best choice. If you travel with your pet to remote areas on a regular basis, you may want to become certified in pet first aid and pet CPR. Many local animal organizations like the Humane Society and SPCA offer affordable training classes.

The Harry F. Byrd Sr. Visitor Center at Milepost 51 on Skyline Drive features exhibits, videos, ranger programs, park permits, and a gift shop.

Early human settlers also left a legacy in the mountains, and the park has more than 100 family cemeteries along with ruins of cabins and farms. The Rapidan Camp was built by President and Mrs. Hoover, serving as their "summer White House," an escape from muggy Washington during the dog days of summer.

You'll see wildlife like this big buck at the park, so keep Fido on a leash!

Shenandoah National Park is one of only a handful of national parks that are not only pet friendly, but also allow canines to hike with their humans. Of the more than 500 miles of trails, less than 20 miles are restricted. The park's website has safety tips for four-legged visitors and a dedicated section detailing the wide array of pet-friendly accommodations, from lodges and cabins to campgrounds. If your pal is athletic

Famous Four-Legged Virginians
FDR'S FALA: FIRST DOG OR FIRST FISH?

Perhaps the most famous presidential canine in history, Fala, the Scottish Terrier, was always by President Franklin Roosevelt's side. At the White House, when the president's breakfast tray was delivered, it always included a bone for the furry leader, and at night, Fala slept in a place of honor in a chair at the foot of FDR's bed. He accompanied the president on many trips, from short jaunts in the car to train and boat excursions. He even attended the Atlantic Charter Conference and the Quebec Conferences during World War II. Both the president and Fala loved the water, and on one fishing trip, Fala learned a new trick. He saw freshly caught fish flopping around on the boat deck and thought it looked like fun, so he started to flip-flop around, and for days afterward, he amused his human with this new trick.

and adventurous, you'll find hours of outdoor activities to enjoy. Dogs must be on a six-foot leash at all times, and be aware that you will encounter all types of wildlife, so keep a close eye and firm hold on canines that have a disposition for hunting. It's also advisable to stick to the easier trails when taking your pooch along, as rocky or difficult hikes can injure your pal's paws, and be sure to carry water and first aid supplies for both yourself and your furry friend.

Getting to the Park and Getting Around

Since there is no air, bus, or rail service into the park, even if you fly into a nearby airport (Dulles International or Charlottesville-Albemarle), you'll still need to rent a car. There are four entrances to the park:

Front Royal: in the north via I-66 from Washington, DC, or Route 340 and Highway 55 (MM 0.6)

Thornton Gap: via US 211 (MM 31.5)

Swift Run Gap: via US 33 (MM 65.7)

Rockfish Gap: southernmost entrance via I-64 or US 250 (MM 104.7). This is also the northern entrance to the Blue Ridge Parkway.

The park's website has excellent directions—GPS and mapping services can be difficult to use given the park's nontraditional addresses. Concrete mile markers on the right-hand side of Skyline Drive run from north to

Pets-in-the-Park Safety Tips

Endurance: Make an honest assessment of your pet's health and endurance before choosing a trail to hike. Remember that your pet needs hydration as much as you do; carry sufficient water and a bowl for frequent water breaks. Also check your pal's paws frequently for abrasions, stickers, or cuts. If your dog tolerates them, doggy hiking boots will cut down on pad injuries.

Wildlife Encounters: You will encounter a variety of wildlife, from snakes, rabbits, squirrels, and chipmunks to deer, bear, and bobcat. How will your pet react? If you have a dog with hunting tendencies, or who is not extremely well trained, think twice about taking them into the wilderness. You may want to use a harness or martingale, rather than a traditional collar, for better control.

Emergency Plan: Have a plan and first aid supplies for emergencies if your pet becomes ill or injured while on a park trail.

Cell Phone: Program the park emergency number (800) 732-0911 into your cell phone.

The deer here seem happy to pose so tourists can snap photos.

Holiday ornaments featuring local wildlife are popular souvenirs at the park.

south, beginning with Mile 0 at the US 340 junction. The posted speed limit is 35 MPH, and watch out for animals crossing the roads, as well as sharp curves. Skyline Drive has 75 scenic overlooks, as well as stop-offs where you can pick up food, gas, and souvenirs. There are two official visitor centers: Dickey Ridge (MM 4.6), 4 miles south of the Front Royal entrance, is open from April to late November. The Harry F. Byrd Sr. Visitor Center (MM 51) is open from late March through late November. You can pick up the official park

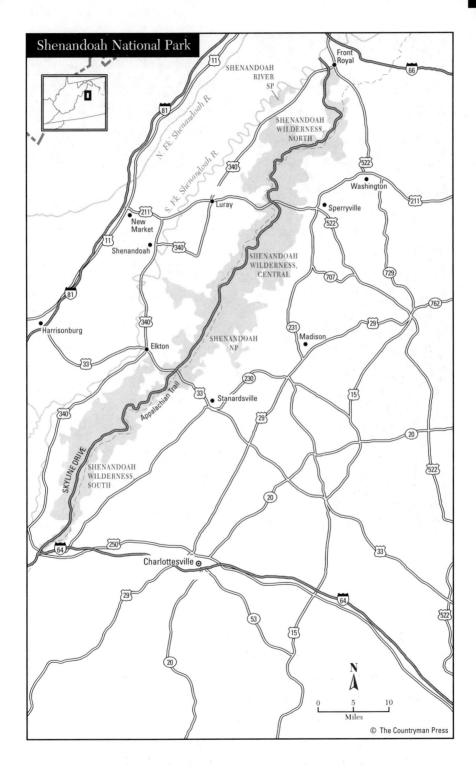

Shenandoah National Park

© The Countryman Press

At any time of day, you'll find visitors reading and relaxing in the spacious lounge at Big Meadows.

visitor guide, *Shenandoah Overlook,* as well as backcountry permits, souvenir passport stamps, and a variety of maps and hiking guides. Entrance fees are waived for holders of a National Parks and Federal Recreational Lands Pass. If you don't have an annual pass, the entrance fee is $15 from March through November per vehicle and $10 from December through February, valid for six days from the date of purchase.

Gas and supplies are available at Elkwallow Wayside (MM 24.1), Big Meadows Wayside (MM 51.2), and Loft Mountain Wayside (MM 79.5).

Best Beds: Comfy Sleeps for You and Your Canine Family

You have several choices for accommodations at Shenandoah National Park. All reservations are made through the park's central reservation system, either online or by phone (888-896-3833; www.visit shenandoah.com). Rates vary by season, starting at an average of $150 per night. A deposit equivalent to one night's room and tax is required at booking. Check the website for special package offers during off-peak times. Book up to a year in advance to get your choice of accommodations in peak seasons like summer and fall.

Pets are welcome with an additional $25 per night/per pet non-refundable cleaning fee, but they are not allowed in the public buildings and must be on a six-foot leash at all times outside of your room. If pets are left alone in a room, they must be crated, and there is two-pets-per-room limit. You can also camp with your four-legged friend at the park's four campgrounds (Mathews Arm, Loft Mountain, Lewis Mountain, and Big Meadows) from $15 per night.

Full-service dining outlets are located at Big Meadows Lodge and Skyland Resort. If you're staying in a cabin with kitchen facilities, you can purchase supplies at one of the camp stores or bring them along.

Camp stores at the park carry a wide variety of supplies, serve food, and have a gift shop.

Fido's Park Packing List

Pet First Aid Kit: The American Veterinary Medicine Association (AVMA) has an excellent, printable list for putting together a pet first aid kit (www.avma.org/firstaid/supplies.asp). Here are some of the basics to include:

Gauze, nonstick bandages, and adhesive tape (do not use human Band-Aids on a dog)

Tweezers for tick/sticker removal

Milk of magnesia (can absorb poison—contact the poison control center before administering)

Eyedropper

Muzzle (injured dogs may bite)

Stretcher (can use a blanket, board, floor mat)

Medications: pack enough of your pet's medications for the entire trip

Food and bottled water: while supplies are available in the park, choices are limited, so bring plenty of your dog's favorite food and bottled water to take on walks and hikes. Also pack a collapsible water bowl to take on outings.

Travel Crate: you must put your dog in a crate if you're leaving your room.

Beds, bowls, and toys: the park does not offer any doggy amenities, so bring your pal's favorites from home.

Moist towelettes and brush: there are no dog spas or groomers in the park so it's up to you to keep your pet clean. Brush daily and check thoroughly for ticks.

Big Meadows has several different buildings in addition to the rooms in the main lodge.

Cabins in the original part of Big Meadows Lodge are tiny and rustic.

Big Meadows Lodge, MM 51.2; open May 16 to November 4. Built in the 1930s by the CCC using stone from Massanutten Mountain and native oak and chestnut for interior finishes and paneling, Big Meadows Lodge has both traditional rooms and suites in multiunit buildings, as well as cabins. Pet-friendly rooms, some with fireplaces, are located in the units across from the main lodge, just a short walk across the parking area. The main lodge features the Spottswood Dining Room, a great room with a stone fireplace and plenty of seating for reading or playing board games, and a spacious terrace with gorgeous mountain views. The Craft Shop serves Starbucks coffee throughout the day and sells park souvenirs and local crafts, and the New Market Tap Room in the lower level of the lodge features live entertainment and light fare in a pub atmosphere. The lodge is named for

the large grassy meadow nearby, and you'll often see deer grazing in the mornings and evenings. Rooms are cozy and comfortable, but do not have telephones or Internet service, although free Wi-Fi is available in the lodge's great room.

Lewis Mountain Cabins, open May 16 to November 4. Rustic, furnished cabins in a secluded wooded area give you and your pooch a chance to slow down and commune with nature. Outdoor grills and picnic tables are provided for alfresco dining.

Skyland Resort, MM 41.7; open March 29 to November 23. Built in 1888 as the private retreat of George Freeman Pollock Jr., Skyland sits at 3,680 feet, offering

The gift shop at Skyland is the largest one in the park.

Skyland Resort lodge has pet-friendly rooms and a dining room with floor-to-ceiling windows overlooking the mountains.

breathtaking mountain views and cool breezes, along with a variety of rooms and cabins. The Pollock Dining Room in the main lodge serves regional specialties like rainbow trout and mile-high blackberry ice cream pie, and the Mountain Taproom serves up light fare and libations, as well as live music. The gift shop here is by far the largest of the park's shops, stocking local jams and the private-label Shenandoah Park wine, as well as a vast array of clothing and gift items. Rooms at Skyland do not have telephones or Internet service, but Wi-Fi is available in the lobby and on the restaurant patio.

Things to Do without Fido: Top Park Picks

Basket-Making Workshop: Learn to make a Colonial-style white oak basket in a class led by local artisan Clyde Jenkins. Jenkins uses techniques passed down through generations of mountain craftsmen and classes are geared to beginners. The four-hour workshops are held in Big Meadows Lodge ($45 per person; materials included; check website for event dates).

Horseback Riding: Take a one- or two-hour guided trail ride through the mountains for a different perspective. The stables are located

Big Meadows got its name from this spacious meadow near the camp store.

near the Skyland Resort (from $42.50 per person).

Twilight Hike: See the mountains and meadows by starlight. Offered on Saturdays throughout the summer and early fall, guided three-hour twilight hikes take you through the big meadow as the sun is setting and on an easy ramble through the park under the stars ($10 per person).

Virginia Wine Tastings: Held at both Big Meadows Lodge and Skyland through the spring and summer seasons, each week a different Virginia winery presents its best vintages. Sample assorted cheeses and take home a souvenir glass ($15 per person).

Waterfalls and Wildflowers: See the majesty of the Blue Ridge with the pros on a full-day guided adventure hike. You can purchase separately (from $103 includes lunch) or in a package that includes one night's lodging.

The Shenandoah Valley: From Apples to Battles

For decades, the tranquil Shenandoah Valley, just 75 miles west of the nation's capital, has been a favorite weekend escape for Washington's influential politicians and their power pooches. The valley stretches for more than 200 miles from Winchester, a pivotal city in the Civil War that changed hands 72 times, to Lexington, home of the nation's oldest state-supported military college and regular stomping grounds of Confederate generals Robert E. Lee and Stonewall Jackson.

While visitors flock to Skyline Drive each fall to see the blazing panorama of color, Beltway insiders know that the fertile valley below holds tantalizing treasures of its own, especially in the spring. Surveyed by a young George Washington, the five-block by two-block town of Little Washington packs a

(Continued on page 183)

A dog-themed float in the Shenandoah Apple Blossom Festival's Grand Feature Parade.
(Winchester-Frederick County Convention & Visitors Bureau)

Fido 411

Here are some of the most important numbers to have when you arrive in the Shenandoah Valley:

✚ 24-hour Emergency Veterinarians

Blue Ridge Veterinary Associates, 120 East Cornwell Lane, Purcellville (540-338-7387; www.blueridgevets.com). This animal clinic offers 24-hour emergency services and is about 51 miles from Luray, VA.

Greenbrier Emergency Animal Hospital, 370 Greenbriar Drive, Charlottesville (434-202-1616; www.greenbrier-emergency.com). Located in Charlottesville, Greenbrier is open 24/7, 365 days a year, including major holidays.

Shenandoah Valley Regional Veterinary Emergency Services, 465 Lee Highway (in the Verona Shopping Center), Verona (540-248-1051; www.svrves.com); Monday to Thursday 6 P.M. to 8 A.M. and Friday 6 P.M. to Monday 8 A.M.

Valley Veterinary Emergency and Referral Center (VVREC), 210 Costello Drive, Winchester (540-662-7811; http://vverc.com). VVREC is the only critical-care animal hospital in the valley, with an onsite surgery, laboratory, and radiation department. More than 50 regional veterinarians refer patients to VVREC for emergency care, and the clinic accepts Care Credit as well as most major credit cards.

Animal Poison Control Center—ASPCA (888-426-4435 or www.aspca .org/pet-care/poison-control/). If you think your pet may have ingested a poisonous substance or animal, help is available 24 hours a day, 365 days a year.

To find an emergency-care veterinarian from your smartphone, check the following websites for the closest location:

www.vetsnearyou.com, www.localvets.com, or **www.animalclinics nearyou.com** Enter the zip code of your location and it will bring up a list and map of the closest veterinarians.

To find a 24-hour pharmacy, check the store-locator search on one of these websites:

CVS: www.cvs.com

Walgreens: www.walgreens.com

RX List: www.rxlist.com/ pharmacy/local_locations_ pharmacies.htm

D-Tails

Visit Winchester www.visit winchesterva.com

Harrisonburg www.harrisonburg tourism.com (check the pet-friendly page for accommodations and pet services)

Staunton www.visitstaunton.com (pronounced STAN-ton)

Lexington www.lexingtonvirginia.com

Shenandoah Valley Travel Association www.visitshenandoah.org

Shenandoah County www.shenandoahtravel.org

Travel 411

The Shenandoah Valley runs for about 200 miles in a predominantly rural region. Specialty pet stores and services are located in the most populated cities of Winchester (north), Harrisonburg (central), and Staunton (south).

Route 11 outside Winchester is a great place to go antiquing.

punch, with its tony antiques shops and boutiques and an internationally renowned inn and restaurant. Winchester was home to the legendary country music star Patsy Cline, and there are numerous country charms in this farming region known as the apple capital of America. Quirky antiques stores filled with Americana that once tempted former First Lady Jacqueline Kennedy, several excellent Virginia vineyards, and a bountiful farmers market are just a few of the local attractions you and Fido will want to explore. Winchester celebrates the blooming of the fragrant and fruitful apple trees with an annual Apple Blossom Festival, while in Harrisonburg and Dayton, Mennonites who settled the region in the early 18th century still drive black horse-drawn buggies. Staunton, the birthplace of Woodrow Wilson and home of his presidential library and museum, is also the location of the world's only re-creation of Shakespeare's indoor playhouse, Blackfriars.

You can do as much or as little as you want in the Shenandoah Valley . . . this is a place for meandering, not multitasking, a warm and welcoming retreat cradled in the arms of the Blue Ridge Mountains. From geological treasures like Natural Bridge to the battlegrounds that divided the nation, the Shenandoah Valley is fertile ground for both food and food for thought, with abundant opportunities for you and Fido to make your own discoveries.

The beautiful and rural Shenandoah County offers plenty of outdoor adventures year-round for you and your pooch. (Courtesy of Shenandoah County Tourism)

Getting Around the Valley

From the Washington, DC, area, Interstate 66 heads west to the Shenandoah Valley, with Little Washington just 60 miles away. I-66 passes through Front Royal and meets I-81 and US 11 at the northern end of the valley, continuing all the way down to the Roanoke Valley at the southern end. I-64 runs east to west and connects Charlottesville to both I-81 and US 11, and SR 39, which takes you into Bath County and the Allegheny Highlands of Virginia, connects with I-81 just north of Lexington. From the southwest tip of Virginia, I-77 crosses I-81 at Wytheville.

The interstates will get you to one of the four major population centers in the Shenandoah Valley—Winchester, Harrisonburg, Staunton, and Lexington—but you'll need to get off the highway and take one of the local highways to explore the region.

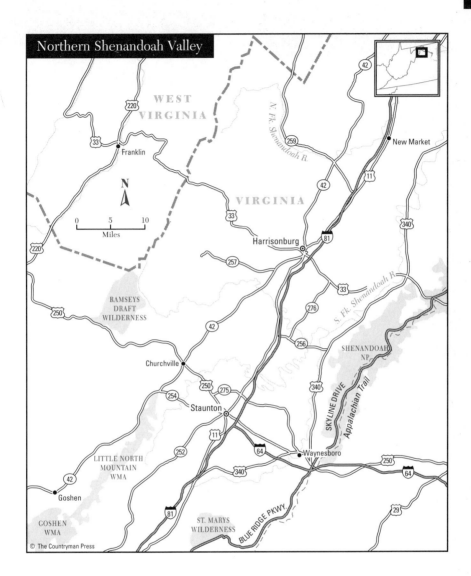

Northern Shenandoah Valley

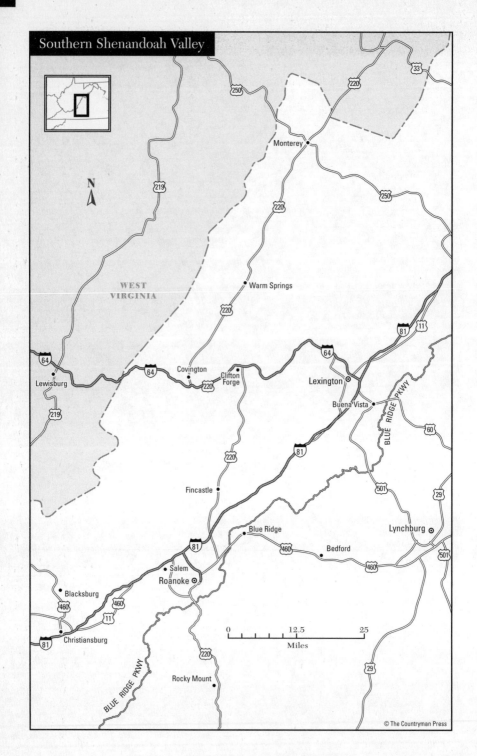

Southern Shenandoah Valley

WEST VIRGINIA

Monterey

Warm Springs

Lewisburg

Covington

Clifton Forge

Lexington

Buena Vista

BLUE RIDGE PKWY

Fincastle

Blue Ridge

Lynchburg

Bedford

Salem

Roanoke

Blacksburg

Christiansburg

Rocky Mount

BLUE RIDGE PKWY

0   12.5   25
Miles

© The Countryman Press

Best Beds: Comfy Sleeps for You and Your Canine Family

Aloft, 1055 Millwood Pike, Winchester (540-678-8899; www .starwoodhotels.com); from $76 per night. Part of the W Hotel Group, Aloft is hip rather than historic, with bright and airy modern rooms that are tech-savvy and stream-lined. You can stay plugged in anywhere in the hotel, with Wi-Fi in the uber-sleek lobby, groovy lounge, and even in the splash pool with its cool pod loungers. Standard amenities include a 42-inch flatscreen, complimentary bottled water, coffee and tea, free Wi-Fi and wired Internet, and

Staunton's main shopping and dining street is just a block from the Stonewall Jackson Hotel.

spa-worthy bath amenities. Aloft is also forward thinking where your furry family is concerned: their Animals Are Fun (ARF) program provides a dog bed, bowl, woof-alicious treats, and toys. Dogs under 40 pounds are welcome under the standard pet policy with no additional fees; if your pal weighs more than 40 pounds, contact the hotel directly to see if they will make an exception.

Natural Bridge Hotel and Conference Center, 15 Appledore Lane, Lexington (540-291-2121; www.naturalbridgeva.com); from $72–82 per night. The official hotel for the area's most popular attraction is located just across the street and welcomes pets in its cottage rooms for an additional fee of $15 per night. Packages are available that include breakfast or admittance to area attractions and activities.

Residence Inn by Marriott, 1945 Deyerle Avenue, Harrisonburg (540-437-7426; www.marriott.com/hotels/travel/shdhr-residence-inn-harrisonburg/); from $139 per night. Pets are welcome to make themselves at home in one of the 108 spacious suites, with a $100 nonrefundable cleaning fee. This is a convenient location if you're traveling to or from Shenandoah National Park: it's just 18 miles west of the Swift Run Gap entrance.

Salamander Resort & Spa, Middleburg (540-687-3600; www.salamanderresort.com); from

The pet-friendly Salamander Resort & Spa in Middleburg, featuring an equestrian center, will open in the summer of 2013. (Courtesy of Salamander Hospitality)

The historic Stonewall Jackson Hotel welcomes four-legged visitors and is within walking distance of downtown shops and restaurants.

easement to ensure tranquility for future generations. Four-legged guests, from horses to canines, are welcome at the resort.

Stonewall Jackson Hotel, 24 South Market Street, Staunton (540-885-4848; www.stonewall jacksonhotel.com); from $179 per night. Located in the heart of downtown within walking distance of shops, restaurants, and attractions, this 1928 historic gem has been elegantly restored, with modern amenities like an indoor pool, fitness center, and Wi-Fi, while retaining its Old World period charm. Your furry friend is welcome, with a flat $50 fee per stay and no weight limits.

$295 per night; call for pet policy details. Scheduled to open in the summer of 2013, this ultra-luxurious resort, spa, and equestrian center will be one of the first to achieve LEED (Leadership in Energy and Environmental Design) certification. Set on 340 acres in the heart of Virginia's horse country, the resort will include a 23,000-square-foot spa, a full-service equestrian center, fine dining featuring the best of Virginia Piedmont cuisine, a cooking studio, wine bar, and 168 elegant rooms and suites. Designed to blend seamlessly with the stunning countryside, 252 acres of the property have been placed in a conservation

This cozy lounge off the lobby of the Stonewall Jackson Hotel showcases the hotel's rich history.

Best Bowls:
Restaurants Worth
a Sitter

L'Auberge Provençale, 13630 Lord Fairfax Highway, Boyce (540-837-1375; www.laubergeprovencale.com). A taste of Provence is the last thing you would expect to find in the tiny town of White Post, but this celebrated bed & breakfast has become a dining destination in its own right. Chef Alain Borel has long been a favorite of the nearby Washington foodie set, and the menu at L'Auberge Provençale changes seasonally; Borel sources as much food as possible from the bounty of the valley, as well as utilizing herbs and fruits and vegetables grown on the property. With a superb wine list, the Chef's Tasting Dinner, a five-course journey with wine pairings, is a worthy splurge. A sample menu includes artichoke ravioli with a balsamic reduction and lemon butter, torchon of foie gras with blackberry gelée and ligonberry salsa, risotto with local asparagus, spring morels and truffle oil, pork belly with beet purée, lamb osso bucco, and a soufflé for dessert. Reservations are required.

The Dancing Goat, the George Washington Hotel, 103 East Picadilly Street, Winchester (540-771-2727; www.dancinggoat restaurant.com). Located in the

Staunton is filled with lovely Victorian-era homes and students from Mary Baldwin college.

historic George Washington Hotel, the Dancing Goat is anything but old fashioned. Priding itself on sourcing local produce and meats, the restaurant's entrées include updated versions of classics, like the local pork chop with tomatillo and green apple sauce. The website offers a nostalgic glimpse into the past with the historic menu from the hotel's early years, when calf sweetbreads with Smithfield Bacon would only set you back $1.25. The prices may have increased, but this is still one of the best eateries in town.

Emilio's, 23 East Beverley Street, Staunton (540-885-0102; www .emiliositalianrestaurant.com). Spread over three floors of a wonderful old downtown building in the heart of the historic district, Emilio's has been a local favorite for more than a decade. A native Italian, Emilio Amato serves up classics from osso buco alla Milanese to calamari fra diavolo in an elegant atmosphere. In the winter, you'll want to cozy up in front of one of the four fireplaces or warm up with a drink in the Pompei Lounge on the third floor.

The Inn at Little Washington, 309 Middle Street, Washington (540-675-3800; www.theinnatlittle washington.com). Lauded by both national and international food critics, Chef Patrick O'Connell's New American cuisine is so sought after

that you must reserve well in advance to enjoy his dazzling creations in the intimate 30-table dining room. A 14,000-bottle wine cellar complements the innovative offerings that change seasonally: late spring and early summer dishes might include pecan-crusted soft shell crab tempura, macaroni and cheese with Virginia ham and shaved black truffle, or a warm salad of pomegranate-molasses-glazed squab. A coveted spot in the kitchen at one of O'Connell's two Chef's Tables will run you $350 (per table) on weekdays and up to $475 on weekends. Prix fixe dinners range from $158–188, excluding tax, gratuity, and beverages.

Southern Inn, 37 South Main Street, Lexington (540-463-3612; http://southerninn.com). Big band–era musicians like Gene Krupa and Tommy Dorsey would always eat here when they were playing nearby. Established in 1932, the Southern Inn was totally renovated by the current owners, George and Sue Ann Huger, maintaining the historical integrity of the building while adding a modern touch. Serving lunch and dinner, the Southern Inn puts classic Virginia dishes like fried chicken and Highland County rainbow trout alongside continental-inspired selections like a locally sourced duck breast with bread pudding, braised greens, and strawberry-rhubarb chutney.

Tail Waggers: Fido's Favorite Outings

Arboretum of Virginia, 400 Blandy Farm Lane, Winchester (540-837-1758; www.virginia.edu /blandy); free; open daily dawn to dusk. About 9 miles east of Winchester, the Arboretum has walking trails throughout its 170 acres of native trees and shrubs, herb gardens, and the most extensive boxwood collection in North America. Four-legged visitors on leashes are welcome to explore this lovely area or picnic with their companions.

Cyrus McCormick's Farm, 128 McCormick's Farm Circle, Raphine (540-377-2255; www.arec.vaes.vt .edu/shenandoah-valley); free; daily 8–5. Pack a picnic for a day on the historic farm where Cyrus McCormick revolutionized farming with the invention of the first reaper. The 634-acre farm, now a part of Virginia Tech University, has a blacksmith shop, gristmill, museum, and picnic area.

Douthat State Park, 14239 Douthat State Park Road, Clifton Forge (540-862-8100; www.dcr .virginia.gov/state_parks/dou .shtml); admission from $4. One of Virginia's six original state parks that opened in 1936 and on the National Register of Historic Places, Douthat is nestled in the Allegheny Highlands. With miles of pet-friendly trails past waterfalls and mountain overlooks, and a 50-acre lake for fishing, Douthat consistently ranks in the top as one of Virginia's favorite parks. Leashed pets are welcome throughout the park, and in cabins (extra $10-per-night pet fee) and campgrounds ($5-per-night pet fee).

Marker-Miller Farm Market, 3035 Cedar Creek Grade (540-662-1391; www.markermillerorchards.com). Purveyor to some of the best chefs in the region, Marker-Miller's farmers market and orchards welcome you and Fido to browse and sniff out the best of locally grown produce, as well as jams, jellies, and baked goods. Munch an apple cider doughnut as you stroll the market or pick your own apples from their orchards in the fall.

New Market Battlefield State Historical Park, 8895 George Collins Parkway, New Market (540-740-3101; www.vmi.edu/new market); $7 grounds tour. You and Fido can tour this 260-acre park where the Confederates were victorious in 1864 with the help of 257 Virginia Military Institute cadets, although your pal can't go inside the museum or attend the battle reenactment in May.

Old Town Winchester Loudoun Street Pedestrian Mall, 1 North Loudoun Street (540) 722-7575; www.oldtownwinchester.com). Located within the 45-block

The Battle of New Market raged around the Bushong House while three generations of the family hid in the basement. (Courtesy of Shenandoah County Tourism)

Historic Register district, the pedestrian mall has been the center of commerce in Winchester for more than two centuries. Filled with outdoor cafés, local boutiques, and historic attractions including Stonewall Jackson's Headquarters Museum, George Washington's Office Museum, and the Old Courthouse Civil War Museum, the mall is also home to the town's special events, from farmers markets to concerts.

Patsy Cline Driving Tour: The historic town of Winchester is widely known as the birthplace of one of country music's most beloved stars, Patsy Cline. The native, who once worked at the local drugstore, hit the big time when she won the Arthur Godfrey talent show, but died tragically in a plane crash at the peak of her career in 1963. Cline is buried in Winchester's Shenandoah Memorial Park, where a bell tower was erected in her honor. Pick up a flyer for a self-guided driving tour of Patsy sites at the Winchester-Frederick County Visitor Center (1400 South Pleasant Valley Road) and pop in your greatest-hits CD.

Veramar Vineyard, 905 Quarry Road, Berryville (540-955-5510; www.veramar.com); $7 tasting. This 100-acre family-owned winery and vineyard loves four-legged visitors. Every summer, Veramar hosts a Dog Days event with complimentary treats for canines, and special wine-tasting events for their humans. Hailing from the Italian Alps,

Although Fido can't go inside the Woodrow Wilson Presidential Library and Museum, he's welcome to stroll the lovely grounds and peek in the windows.

the Bogaty family produces stellar reds and whites that get raves from oenophiles-in-the-know at *Wine Enthusiast* magazine. The family, pioneers of vinifera grape growing in Virginia, also takes sustainability seriously, conscious of preserving the land for future generations.

☻ Sweet Treats and Canine Chic: Where to Shop with your BFF

Glen's Fair Price, 227 North Main Street, Harrisonburg (540-434-8272; www.glensfairprice.com). This is a true variety store and has been a fixture in downtown Harrisonburg since 1941. In addition to general merchandise, if you need a costume for your pet, you can find one here!

Home Farm Store, 1 East Washington Street, Middleburg (540-687-8882; www.homefarm store.com). Spoil your pooch with a stop at the retail outlet for Ayrshire Farm (www.ayrshirefarm .com), consistently awarded the Virginia's Finest products seal, and the place to buy the Furry Foodie brand pet food. Ayrshire's organic raw pet food is made from the same humanely raised beef, poultry, and pork used in their products for humans.

Posh Pets Boutique, 16 South Loudoun Street (540-722-7213; www.oldtownwinchesterva.com /business-directory/shopping/ specialty-shops-boutiques/posh-pets-boutique/). Located on the Old Town Pedestrian Mall, Posh Pets offers locally baked treats, furry fashions, eco-friendly beds, and a vast array of travel accessories.

Wylie Wagg, 5 East Washington Street, Middleburg (540-687-8727; www.wyliewagg.com). If your pal needs premium dog food, Wylie Wagg stocks all of the top organic and holistic brands in dry, canned, and raw forms, as well as a full array of pet accessories. Pick up a few paw-print cookies while you're there!

◉ Big-Box Stores

Petco www.petco.com, 93 S. High Street, Harrisonburg (540-434-4601); 850 Statler Boulevard, Staunton (540-885-8083); 370 Gateway Drive, Winchester (540-667-0562)

PetSmart www.petsmart.com, 1671 E. Market Street, Harrisonburg (540-432-6460); 2310 Legge Boulevard, Winchester (540-662-5544)

♛ A Day of Beauty and Play Dates: Best Pooch Primping and Doggy Daycare

NOTE: Many of these local establishments don't have websites, but have been recommended by the local visitor's bureau. Many big-box stores like Petco and PetSmart also

Meems Bottom Bridge in Mount Jackson, built in 1892 and still in use today, is one of the most photographed attractions in Shenandoah County. (Courtesy of Shenandoah County Tourism)

offer grooming services, and some PetSmart locations offer doggy day care.

Aberdeen Acres Pet Care Center, 667 Walters Mill Lane, Winchester (540-667-7809; www.aberdeen acres.com); from $18 by weight. Nestled in the rolling hills surrounding Winchester, about 4 miles from the downtown district, Aberdeen Acres offers spacious, climate-controlled canine suites with individual outdoor runs for both daycare and overnight boarding, and also has a full-service grooming facility and custom kitchen for finicky eaters.

All Sizes Pet Sitting, Staunton (540-886-3480; www.allsizespet sitting.com); free estimate based on location and hours. Amanda Riesmeyer, who has never met an animal she didn't love, offers pet sitting for all kinds of four-legged furry friends in the Shenandoah Valley area.

Puppy Luv, 4110 Greenmount Road, Harrisonburg (540-833-6901); daycare from $10.

Rocking Horse Doggie Daycare and Boarding, 3459 North Lee Highway, Lexington (540-463-1100; www.rockinghorsepets.com); from $18. This cage-free daycare facility limits the number of dogs onsite, so it's imperative to make a reservation in advance. They also offer grooming services if your pooch needs a bath or a trim.

Additional Grooming Salons

PJ's Pet Palace and Spa, 813 Chicago Avenue, Harrisonburg (540-434-2888).

Wilma and Donna's Pet Paradise, 3015 South Main Street, Harrisonburg (540-432-0770).

Worth a Sitter: Sights to See without Fido

Belle Grove Plantation, 336 Belle Grove Road, Middletown (540-869-2028; www.bellegrove.org); $5; April to October; guided tours every hour at 15 minutes past the hour (10:15, 11:15, 12:15, etc.). Just 6 miles south of Winchester, Belle Grove is the only antebellum plantation in the region. Built in 1797

Belle Grove, the home of James Madison's sister, was at the center of the Battle of Cedar Creek during the Civil War.

from limestone quarried on the property, Belle Grove was the home of Major Isaac Hite and his wife, Nelly Madison (James Madison's sister). In later years, Union general Philip Sheridan used the house as his headquarters during the Battle of Cedar Creek, part of which was fought on the farm itself.

Blackfriars Playhouse, 10 South Market Street, Staunton (540-851-1733; www.americanshakespeare center.com); from $35. The critically acclaimed American Shakespeare Company performs the playwright's classics in this re-creation of the first indoor theater in the English-speaking world. The company performs under the same conditions that would have been present during Shakespeare's day.

Luray Caverns, 101 Cave Hill Road, Luray (540-743-6551; www.luray caverns.com); $24; open daily. One of Virginia's most popular natural landmarks, the caverns, located deep below the Blue Ridge Mountains, are home to the unique Stalacpipe Organ, and majestic cathedral-sized rooms with 10-story-high ceilings.

Natural Bridge, 15 Appledore Lane, Natural Bridge (540-291-2121; www.naturalbridgeva.com); from $19 bridge and $28 combo with caverns. Located on land once owned by Thomas Jefferson, this National Historic Landmark was created by Mother Nature rather than mankind. The scenic trail takes you along Cedar Creek, through the 20-story limestone arch, past Monacan Village, and down to Lace Falls. Spelunkers will want to see the Natural Bridge Caverns, some of the deepest on the East Coast. At dusk, symphonic music and lighting transform the bridge in the *Drama of Creation* celebration (April through October and winter weekends).

Museum of the Shenandoah Valley, 901 Amherst Street, Winchester (540-662-1473; www .shenandoahmuseum.org); $6–10; museum and gardens open 10 A.M. to 4 P.M. Tuesday through Sunday; house closed for preservation until 2014. The 50,000-square-foot museum was designed by Michael Graves, but don't let the modern exterior fool you. Inside, four centuries of history are interpreted through artifacts, multimedia presentations, and displays of fine and decorative arts. The 1736 Glen Burnie House was the home of Winchester's founder, Colonel James Wood, and is surrounded by 25 acres of formal gardens.

Woodrow Wilson Presidential Library and Museum, 18 North Coalter Street, Staunton (540-885-0897; www.woodrowwilson.org); $5–14; check website for hours of operation. Explore Woodrow Wilson's birthplace and home, immerse yourself in World War I history in the trench exhibit that simulates a soldier's experience with lights and sound, or stroll through the magnificent boxwood gardens.

The Woodrow Wilson complex includes the library, museum, gift shop, and his birthplace.

The Roanoke Valley and Virginia's Blue Ridge: Outdoor Adventures and the Star City of the South

C radled by Virginia's Blue Ridge Mountains, the Roanoke Valley is hidden from view on Interstate 81, except for the giant star atop Mill Mountain. Originally intended to be a holiday decoration, the lighted mountaintop star was dedicated in 1949 by Roanoke native John Payne, who played Fred Gailey in the classic Christmas movie *Miracle on 34th Street,* but over the years it became the city icon, earning Roanoke the nickname Star City of the South. Virginia's largest city west of Richmond, Roanoke has an urban flavor with a small-town personality, combining sophisticated cultural attractions like the

(Continued on page 203)

The iconic star atop Mill Mountain looks out over the Roanoke Valley.

(Courtesy of the Roanoke Convention & Visitors Bureau)

Fido 411

Here are some of the most important numbers to have when you arrive in the Roanoke Valley:

✚ 24-hour Emergency Veterinarians

Emergency Veterinary Services of Roanoke (EVS), 4902 Frontage Road (540-563-8575; www.evsroanoke.com). EVS is open evenings, weekends, and holidays for emergency and critical care and has a GPS mapping function on their website so you can get there quickly.

Town & Country Veterinary Clinic, 1605 North Franklin Street, Christiansburg (540-382-5042). Open 24/7, this emergency clinic is a good choice if you're in the New River Valley region.

Animal Poison Control Center—ASPCA (888-426-4435 or www .aspca.org/pet-care/poison-control/). If you think your pet may have ingested a poisonous substance or animal, help is available 24 hours a day, 365 days a year.

To find an emergency-care veterinarian from your smartphone, check the following websites for the closest location:

www.vetsnearyou.com, www.localvets.com, or **www.animalclinics nearyou.com** Enter the zip code of your location and it will bring up a list and map of the closest veterinarians.

24-hour Pharmacies

To find a 24-hour pharmacy, check the store-locator search on one of these websites:

CVS: www.cvs.com

Walgreens: www.walgreens.com

RX List: www.rxlist.com/pharmacy/local_locations_pharmacies.htm

D-Tails

Blue Ridge Parkway (828-298-0398; (www.nps.gov/blri/planyourvisit /roadclosures.htm)

Roanoke Convention and Visitors Bureau www.visitroanokeva.com

Visit Botetourt www.visitbotetourt.com

Visit Floyd www.visitfloyd.org

The Crooked Road www.thecrookedroad.org

Travel 411

During the winter months, portions of the Blue Ridge Parkway may be closed. The city of Roanoke is easy to navigate, with many of the attractions in the central core, so you can park and walk, and there's also a free trolley. Other counties in this region include Botetourt (pronounced BOT-uh-tot), Craig, and Franklin. Attractions in Floyd, Salem, Lexington, and on the Blue Ridge Parkway are easy day trips.

Roanoke has a free trolley service that will take you all over town.

world-class Taubman Museum of Art with the down-home hospitality of the Roanoker Restaurant, with its famous biscuits. Poised between the Blue Ridge Parkway and the Appalachian Trail, the city is the metropolitan hub of Virginia's southwest region, and is a perfect location for exploring the natural abundance of outdoor adventures in Virginia's Blue Ridge.

Spend a morning meandering around Roanoke's Market Street, with its pet-friendly vendors and eclectic shops, or take your four-

See historic steam engines at the Virginia Museum of Transportation.

Fabulous Fidos enjoy being on StarCam at the Roanoke Star atop Mill Mountain.

(Roanoke Valley Convention & Visitors Bureau)

legged friend for a hike on Mill Mountain to get a live shot of yourselves on the Roanoke StarCam. More than 22 miles of greenways, as well as an off-leash dog park, offer plenty of in-town exercise, and mountain adventures are just a short drive away. At the Peaks of Otter, the circular path around the lake is an easy and relaxing walk, while fit Fidos may want to try the more strenuous hike to Sharp Top. You can even take your leashed pal on segments of the Appalachian Trail, and there are several pet-friendly stops along the scenic Blue Ridge Parkway, like one of Virginia's largest wineries, Château Morrisette. With a black Labrador retriever as its official emblem, and several canine tour guides on the property, Château Morrisette is all about the dogs: in fact, their website URL is www.thedogs.com, and they have a line of wines benefiting service-dog groups. The gorgeous gift shop and tasting room has a black paw print path, where four-legged visitors are welcomed warmly by both human and canine staff. Black dogs seem to go hand-in-hand with the Blue Ridge . . . at Black Dog Salvage in the Historic Grandin neighborhood, Sally the black Lab greets visitors and escorts them through the 40,000-square-foot warehouse of architectural treasure. During the summer months, catch the annual Woofstock in Elmwood Park in downtown Roanoke or cool off at nearby Smith Mountain Lake, a popular resort destination for water sports and lakeside fun. Take a sidetrip to nearby Floyd and catch a bluegrass show at the Floyd Country Store, one of the venues on Virginia's Crooked Road Heritage Music Trail. In the fall, droves of leaf-peepers head to the scenic Blue Ridge Parkway, and Roanoke dog lovers head to DogtoberFest. And of course, the Star City wouldn't forget Fido at Christmas, hosting a special pet parade as part of the holiday festival events on Market Square. Railroad buffs will love the Virginia Museum of Transportation and the O. Winston Link Museum of spectacular train photography, and you and your pal can walk along the Rail Walk to play with the working signal lights. Once known as Big Lick, Roanoke was the headquarters for the Norfolk & Western Railway; the coming of the railroad in the 1850s forever changed the sleepy little town into the major metropolitan city of today. When the railroad departed, Roanoke continued to grow and reinvent itself as a burgeoning center for the medical industry and an attractive vacation destination in the heart of Virginia's Blue Ridge.

Diesel jumping off the dock at Smith Mountain Lake.

The Blue Ridge Parkway

One of the top 10 scenic drives in America, the Blue Ridge Parkway stretches from Shenandoah National Park in Virginia to the Great Smoky Mountains National Park in North Carolina. The Virginia portion of the 469-mile parkway runs along the crest of the

Nearby and Noteworthy

LEXINGTON AND LYNCHBURG: LEARN MORE ABOUT JEFFERSON AND JACKSON IN TWO HISTORIC TOWNS

Both Lexington and Lynchburg are within an hour's drive of Roanoke or easily accessible from Charlottesville to the north (66 miles from Lynchburg) on Interstate 81 (Lexington is 30 miles south of Staunton). Lexington is home to the Virginia Military Institute, Washington & Lee University, and the historic Stonewall Jackson house. Take a carriage ride around the historic area with the Lexington Carriage Company (www.lex carriage.com) or explore the town on a free guided walking tour, courtesy of the visitor center. Lynchburg, founded by Quaker pacifist John Lynch, boasts 12 sites on the Civil War Trail, including Appomattox Courthouse National Historical Park. Thomas Jefferson kept a vacation home, Poplar Forest, nearby, and the final home of famous orator Patrick Henry is in neighboring Brookneal. The Booker T. Washington National Monument (www.nps.gov/bowa), honoring the African American educator who founded the Tuskegee Institute, is also worth a visit, as is the home of Harlem Renaissance poet Anne Spencer (www.annespencermuseum.com).

Appomattox Courthouse, SR 24 (434-352-8987; www.nps.gov/apco/); $4 per person or $10 per vehicle. Located 25 miles east of Lynchburg, this 1,700-acre historical park contains 27 structures, some original and some reconstructed, to re-create the setting in 1865 when General Robert E. Lee surrendered to General Ulysses Grant to end the Civil War. During the summer, living-history programs are offered daily.

Appalachians like an azure spine down the western part of the state. In the spring, motorists are treated to a display of wildflowers and waterfalls, dogwood and deer; in the fall, the hills are ablaze with autumn color. Over 100 species of birds, along with white-tailed deer, chipmunks, squirrels, oppossums, and raccoons populate the forests along the drive, so the speed limit is a leisurely and safe 45 miles per hour. Winter weather and construction closures are noted on the National Park Service website or by phone (828-298-0398; www.nps.gov/blri/planyourvisit/roadclosures.htm).

Well-behaved dogs on a six-foot leash are welcome in all of Virginia's national park sites and at many attractions along the parkway, although pets are not allowed in or around concession or swimming areas or in public buildings.

Patrick Henry National Memorial at Red Hill, 1250 Red Hill Road, Brookneal (434-376-2044; www.redhill.org); $6. Red Hill was Patrick Henry's last home and burial site. Tour the seven historic buildings overlooking the Staunton River Valley, housing the largest collection of Henry memorabilia in the world. The home has been reconstructed on the original site, and Henry rests in the family cemetery.

Poplar Forest, 1542 Bateman Bridge Road, Forest (434-525-1806; www.poplarforest.org); $14. Thomas Jefferson's personal retreat, Poplar Forest is the first octagonal home in America and illustrates Jefferson's genius as an architect. Ongoing archaelogical excavations on the plantation continue to uncover fascinating insights into Jefferson's life and interests. This national treasure was almost lost after the house passed into private ownership and developers gobbled up the 4,812-acre plantation to build subdivisions, leaving only 50 acres surrounding the main house, and two original outbuildings. In 1983, a small group of local residents formed a nonprofit organization to rescue this presidential retreat, buying back original acreage and restoring the house to its original condition. Ongoing restoration work, land purchases, and archaeological discoveries continue today.

Stonewall Jackson House, 8 East Washington Street, Lexington (540-463-2552; www.stonewalljackson.org); $8. The famous general lived in this house for two years before leaving to command troops during the Civil War. At that time, he was teaching physics and military tactics to cadets at the Virginia Military Institute and pursuing his passion for gardening. The only home he ever owned, Jackson's house displays some of his belongings as well as period furnishings.

Getting Around on the Parkway

Distance is measured by mileposts (MM), beginning with zero at the Rockfish Gap entrance (the northern end where Skyline Drive ends and the parkway begins) to MM213 at the Blue Ridge Music Center, where the Virginia portion of the Blue Ridge Parkway ends. Be sure to start out with a full tank of gas, as there are few opportunities along the route to purchase fuel.

Highlights and Attractions along the Parkway

In addition to the spectacular scenery and wildlife, there are several attractions along the way for you and your best friend to explore.

MM5 to 9.3: Humpback Rocks offers hiking trails to the rocks and self-guided trails through a collection of old Appalachian farm buildings.

Roanoke's annual holiday festival includes a pet parade.

(Roanoke Valley Convention & Visitors Bureau)

MM10.7: At Ravens Roost, panoramic vistas of the mountains and the Shenandoah Valley to the west are a great photo opportunity or a good place to stretch your legs.

MM16: For a longer break from driving, the recreation area at Sherando Lake in the George Washington National Forest is about 4.5 miles off the exit and offers swimming, picnic grounds, and camping.

MM29: Whetstone Ridge, so named for providing generations of mountain men with sharpening stones, has a visitor center and 12-mile trail with amazing views.

MM34.4: At Yankee Horse Ridge, legend has it that a Union soldier's horse fell and had to be put out of its misery. Take a scenic walk to Wigwam Falls to see the reconstructed spur of an old logging railroad.

MM58 to 63.6: Otter Creek winds all the way down the mountains to the James River, while Otter Lake offers recreational fishing.

MM63.8: The Kanawha Canal, planned and surveyed by George Washington, was designed to transport passengers and freight by water from the western counties of Virginia to the coast.

MM71: Petites Gap was named for a local family. Seven miles to the west is Cave Mountain Lake in the Jefferson National Forest, where you can swim, picnic, or camp.

MM83.4: Follow the 1.6-mile loop trail to view Fallingwater Cascades.

MM84 to 87: Peaks of Otter is one of the largest developed sites along the Blue Ridge Parkway, with a lodge, restaurant, visitor center, gift shop, and camping. While the lodge is not pet friendly, the recreational areas are, and there's a wonderful mile-long trail that circles the lake—perfect for a leisurely walk with your pooch.

MM114.9: Follow the trail to see the Roanoke River Gorge.

MM115.1: Although the historic areas of Virginia's Explore Park are currently closed, leashed pets are welcome in the recreation areas, picnic areas, and on the hiking trail, and there is a visitor center on site.

The lake below Sharp Top at the Peaks of Otter has a walking path around it, perfect for a stroll with your pooch.

Famous Four-Legged Virginians
BLACK DOGS IN THE BLUE RIDGE: SALLY THE TV STAR

At Black Dog Salvage, Sally, the co-owner's friendly black Labrador re-triever, guides architectural salvage and antiques hunters through the massive 40,000-square-foot warehouse in Roanoke's picturesque Grandin Village. When *The Nate Berkus Show* filmed a segment at Black Dog Salvage, Sally had a starring role. The namesake of the business, however, was another black Lab named Molly, who lived a full life of more than 13 years, training Sally and working up until her very last day. From garden statuary and cast-iron fencing to Victorian fireplace mantels and stained glass windows, Black Dog has a bit of most bygone eras. A doggone great way to spend a Saturday afternoon!

Sally loves to greet shoppers at Black Dog Salvage in Roanoke.

MM129.6: The Roanoke Valley Overlook gives a panoramic view of the valley, the largest population center along the parkway. You can get to Roanoke via US 220 at MM121, VA 24 (MM112) and US 460 (MM105).

MM167 to 174: At an elevation of 3,572-feet, a formation called Rocky Knob overlooks Rock Castle Gorge. The downhill trail hike here is too steep for four-legged visitors.

MM154.5: Smart View is a perfect place to see Virginia dogwood trees in bloom in the spring, especially near the Trail Cabin built in the late 1800s.

MM176.1: The charming Mabry Mill includes an early 20th century gristmill, sawmill, and blacksmith shop, with demonstrations of these old-time trades.

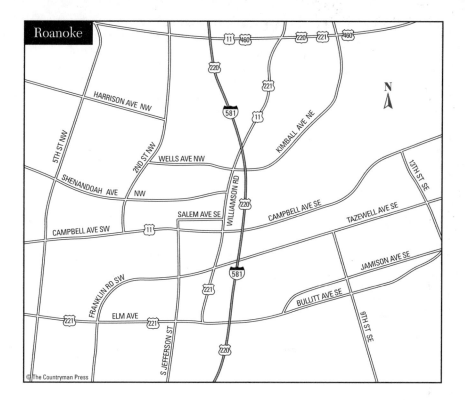

This is one of the most popular and scenic stops along the Virginia section of the Blue Ridge Parkway and a photographer's favorite.

MM188.8: Groundhog Mountain has picnic grounds, an observation tower, and fine examples of several types of rural fences including post and rail, snake, and buck.

MM213: Celebrating the traditional Blue Ridge music and culture, the Blue Ridge Music Center (www.blueridgemusiccenter.org) is the end of the Virginia section of the parkway.

Getting to Roanoke

Interstates 81 and 77 crisscross the Roanoke Valley and the Appalachian Plateau. I-81 runs north-south, as does the Blue Ridge Parkway, which begins at Rockfish Gap in the north. US 460 runs east-west, as does I-64 from Richmond, which meets I-81 at Staunton. Roanoke is about a three-hour drive from Richmond, four hours from Washington, and 49 miles south of Lexington.

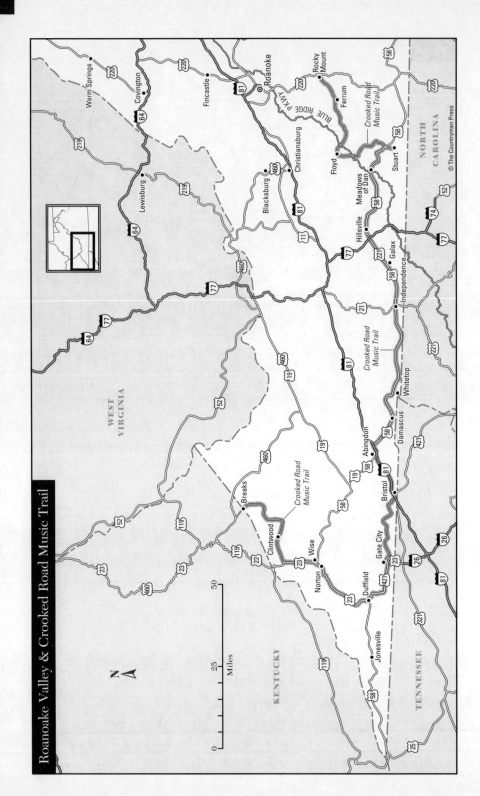

Roanoake Valley & Crooked Road Music Trail

© The Countryman Press

Best Beds: Comfy Sleeps for You and Your Canine Family

Bent Mountain Lodge and Bed & Breakfast, 9039 Mountain View Drive, Copper Hill (540-651-2525; www.bentmountainlodgebedand breakfast.com); from $110 per night. This 15,000-square-foot lodge sits atop a mountain over-looking the Blue Ridge Parkway, close to Roanoke, Floyd, and Salem.

Near Market Square in Roanoke, a canine fountain sets the pet-friendly tone.

Request a cabin suite for you and your furry friend, as they have easy outdoor access as well as an en-closed porch for enjoying the mountain vistas. A continental breakfast is included in the rate, and cabin suites also have access to a centrally located kitchen if you prefer to prepare your own meals.

Brughs Inn, 1226 Lynchburg Turnpike, Salem (540-761-2094; www.brughsinn.com); from $99 per night. Featured on the Salem Historical Society Homes Tour, this small B&B is within walking dis-tance of the Salem Civic Center, Salem Stadium, and the Elizabeth Campus of Roanoke College. Rooms have a gas fireplace, queen bed, flatscreen television, and private bath. Well-behaved pets are wel-come and must be crated in the rooms; pets under 35 pounds are an additional $10 per night, and there is a large-dog fee of $20 per night. A continental breakfast is included in the room rate.

Hotel Floyd, 120 Wilson Street Southeast, Floyd (540-745-6080; www.hotelfloyd.com); from $79.50 per night. A designated Virginia Green Hotel, Hotel Floyd was built and furnished in 2007 with sustain-able materials. Modern amenities and mountain décor give the hotel a comfy vibe, and Fido is welcome with no additional fees in the two special Floyd Humane Society Pet-Friendly Suites, featuring a full

Roanoke's favorite chocolatier, Chocolate Paper, supports the local SPCA and also has some unique doggy treats.

kitchen, flatscreen television, free Wi-Fi, and in-room coffeemaker, as well as an elevated dog bed and food and water bowls for your four-legged roommate. The hotel sponsors a free concert series at the Floyd Country Store on Thursdays, so you also get entertainment included in the room rate!

Mariners Landing Resort and Conference Center, 1217 Graves Harbor Trail, Smith Mountain Lake (540-297-4900; www.mariners landing.com); from $99–299 per night. This 1,000-acre resort on Smith Mountain Lake has three pools, a small beach, a marina with boat rentals, a golf course, and a spa. Furnished rental units have a lovely porch with lake views, and there are restaurants onsite, like Benjamin's at the Pointe, if you don't feel like cooking. Specific units are pet friendly, although the weight limits vary by individual condominium: in general, dogs from 20–80 pounds (no aggressive dogs) are allowed with an additional $15-per-day fee.

Santillane Bed and Breakfast, 99 Housman Street, Fincastle (540-473-3898; www.santillane.com); from $100 per night. This stately manor house has four rooms with romantic, antique double beds and working fireplaces, as well as a larger suite with a library, screened porch, bedroom, and bath. Well-behaved dogs are welcomed with an additional $10-per-night fee and a request that they be crated in the rooms. The 25-acre property has two golden retrievers to welcome your pal and plenty of space to roam.

Sheraton Roanoke Hotel & Conference Center, 2801 Hershberger Road, Roanoke (540-561-7904; www.sheratonroanoke .com); from $109 per night. The elegantly appointed Sheraton Roanoke offers all the modern amenities a traveler could want, as well as indoor and outdoor pools, a fitness center, and onsite dining at Shula's 347 Grill (Fido will want a

doggy bag from this steakhouse favorite!). Your pooch will get a Sheraton Sweet Sleeper Dog Bed, as well as food and water bowls in your room, and the grounds are equipped with several pet stations for easy cleanup. Dogs up to 80 pounds are welcome with no additional fees.

Smith Mountain Lake State Park, 1235 State Park Road, Huddleston (540-297-6066; www.dcr.virginia .gov/state_parks/smi.shtml); from $59 per night cabins; $20 per night camping. You can camp with your pet or snuggle up in a cozy cabin at Smith Mountain Lake State Park. Featuring the state's second-largest freshwater lake, the park also has hiking trails, a fishing pier, boat

Sheraton Roanoke Hotel & Conference Center

rentals, and numerous water activities. Plan on an additional fee of $5 per night for camping and $10 per night for cabins.

Best Bowls: Restaurants Worth a Sitter

Carlos Brazilian International, 4167 Electric Road (540-776-1117; www.carlosbrazilian.com). This hilltop restaurant features international cuisine, with French, Italian, and Spanish classics as well as Brazilian specialties like *moqueca mineira* (shrimp, clams, and white-

Try one of Chef Carlos' Brazilian specialties or choose from an international menu featuring French, Spanish, and Italian favorites.

fish in a Brazilian sauce). The view from the terrace is spectacular, especially at sunset, and the service and food are excellent.

Don Shula's 347 Grill, Sheraton Roanoke Hotel & Conference Center (540-366-5220; www.shulas347 roanoke.com). This is the place for mouthwatering steak in Roanoke, and Fido will give his dinner doggy bag a five-woof rating. The contemporary dining room is usually packed, so reservations are recommended. In addition to the best Black Angus in town, Shula's also features fresh fish daily.

Metro, 14 Campbell Avenue Southeast (540-345-6645; www .metroroanoke.com). Located in the downtown area, this stylish eatery features DIY entrées from custom vegetarian dishes to sushi, sashimi, and dim sum, but this isn't an Asian restaurant. Global food is comfortably paired with Southern favorites like collard greens and bacon, but old favorites are taken to a new level with the addition of truffles to mac 'n cheese or a burger made with Kobe beef. Share a paper cone of Parmesan truffle fries while you wait for your dinner.

The Roanoker, 2522 Colonial Avenue Southwest (540-344-7746; www.theroanokerrestaurant.com). What started out as a lunch counter in downtown Roanoke in 1941 has become the most iconic

Peaks of Otter Winery Horse & Hound Festival

Every summer, the Peaks of Otter Winery hosts the Horse & Hound Wine Festival to benefit area dog and equine rescue groups. More than 10 regional wineries participate in the tasting exhibits, so you'll be able to taste several of Southwest Virginia's finest vintages. Activities include agility dogs, a parade of horses, a muskrat race, arts and crafts, and live entertainment.

www.BedfordWine.com

restaurant in the region over the past seven decades, featured on Al Roker's Food Network television show, *Roker on the Road*. On any given morning, you may see the mayor and other local business leaders meeting over breakfast at this down-home diner, enjoying the famous biscuits that are featured in *Southern Living*'s cookbook.

Wild Flour, 1212 4th Street Southwest (540-343-4543; http://wildflour4thst.com). Located in the Old Southwest Historic district of Roanoke, Wild Flour offers whole foods that are made from the owner's original recipes, with great vegetarian selections as well as meatloaf like Mom used to make. The menu features soups, salads,

and sandwiches and the bakery counter is hard to resist.

Tail Waggers: Fido's Favorite Outings

Off-Leash Dog Park

Roanoke Dog Park in Highland Park, 1212 5th Street SW and Washington Ave SW (www.roanokeva.gov/85256a8d0062af37/vwContentByKey/N2823RCZ255LGONEN). The city's first public dog park within the larger Highland Park has fenced areas for both large and small dogs, Mutt Mitt cleanup bags, fun fire hydrants, and fresh water.

More Tail Waggers

The Appalachian Trail (www.appalachiantrail.org); free. The trail crosses the valley at Troutville, about 5 miles north of Roanoke. McAfee Knob and Dragon's Tooth, two of the most photographed landmarks on the trail, are accessible from SR311 to the west. Dogs are allowed to hike with their humans on most of the trails with a few exceptions detailed on the trail's website (www.appalachiantrail.org/hiking/hiking-basics/hiking-with-dogs).

Carvins Cove Natural Reserve, 9644 Reservoir Road (540-563-9170; www.roanokeva.gov). Located near Hollins College about 8 miles from downtown Roanoke, Carvins

One of the two largest wineries in Virginia, Chateau Morrisette is both a dog- and wine-lovers' paradise.

Cove is the second-largest municipal park in the country, with 12,700 acres of hiking, equestrian trails, and natural beauty including a major water source for the region, the Carvins Cove Reservoir. Rent a boat at the dock or take your pal on one of the many park trails or for a picnic on the grounds.

Château Morrisette Winery, Milepost 171.5, Blue Ridge Parkway, Meadows of Dan (540-593-2865; www.thedogs.com); tours free; tasting $8 (10 wines and souvenir glass); open Monday to Thursday 10–5, Friday and Saturday 10–6, Sunday 11–5. There are black dogs everywhere at Château Morrisette: on the grounds, in the tasting room, and on the wine labels. The

The Chateau Morrisette dogs pose in front of their signature wines.

most pet-friendly winery in the state, as well as one of the largest, not only welcomes canine visitors but also supports animal organizations throughout Virginia with special events like adoption days and through donations from its line of Service Dog wines. Fido is welcome on the grounds and in the tasting room and gift shop (there's some great pup stuff!), but they also have a kennel onsite if you want to relax over lunch in their excellent restaurant. If you visit during the summer or fall, try to catch one of the Black Dog Wine and Music Festivals or a free concert on Sunday afternoon.

Market Square (540-342-2028; www.downtownroanoke.org/city-market). In the heart of Roanoke, the City Market is one of Virginia's oldest continuous farmers markets, and the restored City Market Building also offers a food court and several restaurants. Street vendors, including Paw Paws Homemade Dog Treats, add to the festive atmosphere on Market Street, lined with boutiques and locally owned shops. If your pooch gets thirsty, there's a doggy water fountain right at the top of the street.

Mill Mountain Park and the Roanoke Star, 2198 Mill Mountain Spur (540-342-6025; www.roanoke va.gov/starcam); free. Just 2 miles from downtown following Walnut Street south, the mountaintop park

Black paw prints on the floor lead the way to the elegant tasting bar at Chateau Morrisette.

features miles of pet-friendly hiking trails and, at the 1,703-foot summit, the Roanoke Star and Overlook. The 100-foot star, lighted at night, has a live StarCam, so visitors can email their live shots via cell phone to friends and family back home. You can also access the park from Parkway Spur Road off the Blue Ridge Parkway at MM120.3.

Peaks of Otter Recreation Area, MM86 Blue Ridge Parkway (540-586-4357; www.peaksofotter.com); free. The portion of the Blue Ridge Parkway that leads to the Peaks of Otter is also a state route, so it doesn't close during bad weather like other portions of the scenic road. About 25 miles northeast of Roanoke, this beautiful area includes picnic areas, a multitier waterfall, Fallingwater Cascades, and

hikes to the peaks of the cone-shaped Sharp Top Mountain (3,875 feet) and Flat Top (4,004 feet). If Fido isn't up to the rugged climb, you can take the easy 1-mile trail that loops around Abbott Lake. Pets are allowed on trails and in the campgrounds, but are not permitted in the lodge.

Roanoke Valley Greenways (www.greenways.org). Greenways are scenic connectors that link natural resources to Roanoke's neighborhoods and downtowns, and are perfect for long strolls with your pooch. The Roanoke River Greenway, Lick Run Greenway, Mill Mountain Greenway, Murray Run Greenway, and Tinker Creek Greenway offer a combined 22 miles of hiking fun. Pets must be leashed on the greenways; bring your own cleanup supplies and water.

Paw Paws Homemade Dog Treats is popular with four-legged shoppers on Roanoke's Market Street. (Roanoke Valley Convention & Visitors Bureau)

☺ Sweet Treats and Canine Chic: Where to Shop with Your BFF

Biscuits and Bubbles, 109 W. Main Street, Salem (540-378-5200; http://biscuitsandbubbles.com). Locally owned by the same family who operate the Carvins Cove Bed & Biscuit canine B&B, this self-service dog wash is also a retail store stocking premium pet foods and Paw Paws natural treats.

Nature's Emporium, 3912 Brambleton Avenue (540-989-7735; www.mynaturesemporium.com). Nature's Emporium stocks a wide variety of natural, organic, and raw premium pet foods, as well as all manner of toys and accessories.

Paw Paws (www.pawpawstreats .com). Roanoke Valley's favorite Fido treats are available at the Paw Paws booth at the weekend farmers market and at Biscuits and Bubbles in Salem.

Pet Planet Outfitters, 7956 Forest Edge Drive (866-553-6643; www.pet planetoutfitters.com). If you're looking for a high-tech pet product, you'll find it at Pet Planet, the authorized dealer for DOGTEK, Essential Pet Products, PetSafe, SportDOG Brand, Innotek, and Dog Trakker. They also carry a large line of holistic pet foods and supplies, as well as accessories.

Viva La Cupcake, 1302 Grandin Road (540-204-3100; http://vivala cupcakes.com). Located on the main shopping street in Historic Grandin Village, Viva La Cupcake makes the most decadent desserts in the region, with a wide variety of original flavors and toppings that change daily. Take Fido on a weekend when the owner makes up special Pupcakes for visiting pooches.

Walkabout Outfitter, 301 Market Street (540-777-2727; http://walk aboutoutfitter.com). If you need some hiking gear and trail tips for you and your four-legged friend, drop by Walkabout on Market Street for some local expertise and top-of-the-line gear.

Viva la Cupcake in Historic Grandin makes human cupcakes and all-natural canine pupcakes.

◉ Big-Box Stores

Petco www.petco.com, 630 Brandon Avenue Southwest, Roanoke (540-342-2364)

Petland www.petland.com, 4335 Pheasant Ridge Road, Roanoke (540-776-2890)

PetSmart www.petsmart.com, 4749 Valley View Boulevard Northwest, Roanoke (540-362-2994)

♛ A Day of Beauty and Play Dates: Best Pooch Primping and Doggy Daycare

About Pets Center, 1604 Conehurst Boulevard, Salem (540-986-1604; www.aboutpetscenterresort.com); boarding from $22; daycare from $14. You may miss having your pooch along, but Fido will be in bow-wow heaven at this pet resort with its own salon and spa, Zen Garden, Butterfly Garden, and Doggie Park. There is an extra charge for playtime in the beautifully landscaped Doggie Park ($7 for a 30-minute session with a certified pet-care technician), complete with its own pool and cascading waterfall and agility course. Canine "chateaus" come in a variety of sizes and feature orthopedic beds, soothing music, and hospital-grade air systems.

Aspen Grove Bed & Breakfast, 7373 Franklin Road, Boones Mill (540-776-7656; www.aspengrove boarding.com); boarding from $22; daycare from $13. This doggy B&B is nestled on 30 acres surrounded by the forests of the Blue Ridge, and suites have private 50-square-foot patios for Fido to enjoy the scenery. Four-legged guests are served afternoon tea with gourmet biscuits, and grooming services are also available.

Carvins Cove Bed & Biscuit, 109 West Main Street, Salem (540-384-6736; http://biscuitsandbubbles .com); from $25 per night. This locally owned canine B&B offers Kuranda beds, indoor and outdoor runs, lots of TLC, and Paw Paws homemade treats at turndown.

Klub Kanine, 1872 Apperson Drive, Salem (540-389-7674; www.klub kanine.com); boarding from $24; daycare from $12. Specializing in luxury services for small canines 25 pounds and under, Klub Kanine is an award-winning resort and spa offering both overnight stays and daycare, as well as à la carte grooming services. Treat your pal to a Jacuzzi bubble bath and deep massage with heated towels and a comfy robe for after-bath relaxation.

Star City's Bark Avenue, 703 Townside Road Southwest, Roanoke (540-206-2821; www.starcitysbark ave.com). From show cuts and summer shave downs to Mohawks, the groomers at this salon go from traditional to trendy. For a fluffy

The Crooked Road: A Toe-Tapping Trail in Southwest Virginia

Bluegrass, gospel, and old-time country music has deep roots in the hills of southwest Virginia, and the Crooked Road, a 250-mile route that begins in Ferrum and meanders down to the state line in Bristol and back up into the western reaches of the state, has been designated as the state's Music Heritage Trail. From the Friday Night Jamboree at the Floyd Country Store (www.floydcountrystore.com) to the annual Old Fiddlers Convention in Galax (www.oldfiddlersconvention.com), you can tap your toes at a number of venues, visit the Ralph Stanley Museum (www.ralphstanleymuseum.com), or catch a festival at the Carter Family Fold (www.carterfamilyfold.org) or the Blue Ridge Music Center's (www.blue ridgemusiccenter.net) outdoor amphitheater. If you can't make it in person, the Rex Theatre (www.rextheatergalax .com) broadcasts its shows live on WBRF 98.1 (www.thecrookedroad.org).

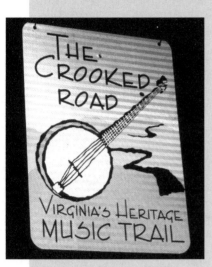

The Crooked Road, Virginia's Heritage Music Trail, runs through the southwestern part of the state.

and healthy coat, choose from a large line of shampoos from papaya and oatmeal to medicated or pH balanced.

Taj Mapaw, 3112 Franklin Road Southwest, Roanoke (540-342-3557; www.taj-ma-paw.com); boarding from $18; daycare from $15. While it may not look like its inspiration, Taj does offer spacious, deluxe kennels with color television and radio for its canine guests, as well as a large play area and lots of one-on-one attention. Watch your dog at play on the live webcam or add on a bath and brush to their day of play.

🐾 Pet Sitters and Dog Walkers

Creature Comfort (540-467-2766; www.mycreaturecomfort.com)

Mad Dog Walking (540-204-8585; www.maddogwalking.com)

Pet Pals (540-797-2363; www.roanokepetsitter.com)

NOTE: Many PetSmart stores also offer grooming and doggy daycare.

Worth a Sitter: Sights to See without Fido

Center in the Square, 1 Market Street (540-342-5700; www.center inthesquare.org); see website for combination ticket pricing. Anchoring Market Square, the Center houses regional museums of science, history, and art, along with the Mill Mountain Theatre and Hopkins Planetarium and a rooftop deck with a butterfly habitat. During the massive renovations of the historic building, individual museums were moved to temporary spaces throughout the city, but all are expected to be under one roof by 2013.

Floyd Country Store, 206 South Locust Street, Floyd (540-745-4563; www.floydcountrystore.com). This quintessential country general merchandise store is also one of the major venues on Virginia's Crooked Road Heritage Music Trail, and features live music Thursday through Sunday. For an authentic jam session, try to catch the Friday Night Jamboree ($5).

O. Winston Link Museum, 101 Shenandoah Avenue (540-982-5465; www.linkmuseum.org); $5; open Monday to Sunday 10–5. Link spent years in the late 1950s and early 1960s photographing the last great steam engines of the Norfolk

The Floyd Country Store is not only fun for shopping, it also hosts live music as part of the Crooked Road Music Trail.

The Floyd Country Store offers nostalgic treats, clothes, and gifts.

& Western Railroad, and decades before special night lighting for photography was invented, he created his own effects using hundreds of light bulbs. The nostalgic black-and-white photos not only evoke the ending of an era, but also pay homage to the role the railroad played in southwest Virginia. A must-see for fans of photography or trains.

Taubman Museum of Art, 110 Salem Avenue (540-342-5760; www.taubmanmuseum.org); $7; Tuesday to Saturday 10–5; free on First Fridays 5–8 P.M. While it's called a museum, the Taubman really considers itself to be an art center: broader in scope than a museum and with exhibitions and educational programs and activities that make it a "town hall" for the arts, as well as a social focal point for the residents of the region. The contemporary architecture of the faceted-glass structure reflects the eclectic exhibitions: a selection of Civil War sketches might sit side-by-side with a collection of sculptures made from found objects. Norah's Café serves light fare, and the museum gift shop is full of quirky treasures.

Virginia Museum of Transportation, 303 Norfolk Avenue (540-342-5670; www.vmt .org); $8; Monday to Saturday 10–5, Sunday 1–5. Close to Market Square, the Virginia Museum of Transportation has a huge collection of diesel and steam locomotives and dozens of original train cars, in addition to model trains and several classic automobiles. You can board some of the train cars, many of which were built in this railroad town. It's easy to imagine the billowing smoke and bellowing whistle as you stand next to one of the behemoth steam engines.

Just hanging out at the Roanoke Star, waiting to be discovered.

(Roanoke Valley Convention & Visitors Bureau)

Index